LAITY STIRRING THE CHURCH

LAITY STIRRING THE CHURCH

DOLORES R. LECKEY

PROPHETIC QUESTIONS

FORTRESS PRESS   **Philadelphia**

LAITY EXCHANGE BOOKS

Library of Congress Cataloging-in-Publication Data

Leckey, Dolores R.
    Laity stirring the church.

    (Laity exchange books)
    1. Church. 2. Laity. 3. Christianity—20th century.
I. Title. II. Series.
BV600.2.L37 1987   270.8′28   86–45213
ISBN 0–8006–1659–6

2544G86   Printed in the United States of America   1–1659

Dedicated
to the memory of Mark Gibbs
a layperson of uncommon grace

Contents

Editor's Introduction

THIS SERIES OF Laity Exchange books is designed to help the Christian laity, in all of our churches, to develop our understanding of how we are called to serve and to minister today.

I am especially pleased that the first Roman Catholic contributor to this series is Dolores Leckey, for I have long admired both her work and her personal lifestyle. She writes on the one hand as a convinced and loyal Catholic: indeed, as Executive Director of the U.S. Bishops' Committee on the Laity she knows more than most people the hard demands which go with such a distinguished official position. She is also a willing and determined "ecumaniac," who delights to report how God has called and blessed men and women in different Christian traditions and churches. And I know nobody who has been more successful in combining these denominational and ecumenical responsibilities with such evident cheerfulness.

More than this: Dolores Leckey has demonstrated in her personal and family and public life how the people of God—clergy and laity together—are called to move ahead on pilgrimage. Her kind of ecumenism is much more than a matter of pleasant conferences on liturgical or historical controversies. She asks us all to learn and to work together, so that we may show forth God's love and generosity, so that we may be more deeply committed to the gospel both in our daily work and in the little but significant details of our family and personal relationships. She writes clearly, pointedly and hopefully. I am sure that this fine book will prove a blessing to its readers.

MARK GIBBS

Acknowledgments

WRITING A BOOK is an example of life in the body of Christ. The writer is only one member of the body. There are so many others who are joined with the writer in the bringing forth of a new book.

My colleagues at the National Conference of Catholic Bishops have been indirectly or directly joined with me in producing this book. Monsignor Daniel F. Hoye, general secretary of the National Conference of Catholic Bishops/United States Catholic Conference, provided, as always, a backdrop of quiet support. Dr. Eugene Fisher, director of the National Conference of Catholic Bishops Catholic-Jewish Secretariat, read the manuscript through an ecumenical/interreligious lens and offered a candid and helpful critique. Ms. Carol Chastain, staff assistant in the Laity Secretariat, willingly went "the extra mile" while the book was taking shape. And Mr. William Kissane, director of the United States Catholic Conference Data Processing Department, helped me with the intricacies of word processing. To all, my deep appreciation for their gifts of time and expertise.

I want to thank, too, Dr. David Thomas, director of the Program for Adult and Christian Community Development at Regis College in Denver, Colorado. His thorough scrutiny of the manuscript, together with his theological reflections and editorial suggestions, greatly influenced the final version.

My husband, Thomas Leckey, provided not only a supportive environment for me to work at this "second full-time job," he provided his labor as well, in the home and at the word processor—and, as always, it was a labor of love.

I also want to thank Harold Rast of Fortress Press for his extraordinary patience and trust as he waited for *Laity Stirring the Church* to come to life, and Mark Gibbs who not only asked me to undertake a book in the Laity Exchange series, but held me to the task with his English wit and Christian perseverance. May he rest in peace, and may he continue to stir Christian laity to demonstrate faith in action.

And finally, my gratitude to the people who are in these pages: the laymen and laywomen who are forging the prophetic questions; and the bishops, priests, and ministers who are making common cause with the laity. Together they are a reminder of the Holy Spirit's energetic and abiding presence in the church.

Introduction

SOMETHING IS STIRRING in the Christian churches. The stirring is deep and steady and patient, and it is producing a nourishment rich in variety but containing the tried and true nutrients of the past. Life-giving and fragrant, the stirring attracts. If you look carefully, you see that someone is doing the stirring. That someone is people, all kinds of Christian people: Catholics and Quakers, Lutherans and Episcopalians, Baptists and Presbyterians, Mennonites and Methodists; young people, old people, white people, people of color, poor people, rich people, people in the middle. They are laypeople, for the most part: neither the ordained people nor the professional people so much—their role is to keep the stirring to a minimum for the sake of tranquility and order— but the world's people, the baptized who are at work in the banks and studios, the offices and classrooms and homes. These people are the church in the world, and they are stirring the old order with the powerful existential questions that have been shaped in the cauldrons of their own lives.

This stirring is part of the effort of people to respond to the fresh, good news that went out from the Second Vatican Council's call for the restoration of unity among all Christians;[1] affirmation of the human/personalist side of marriage;[2] and rejection of "every type of discrimination whether social or cultural, whether based on religion, sex, race, color, social condition, language or religion."[3]

That was not all. People everywhere heard the universal call to holiness. "All . . . of whatever rank or status are called to the fullness of the Christian life and to the perfection of charity."[4] This was a clear

13

affirmation that neither class distinction nor elitism has a place within the church. The communitarian character of the gospel was sounded as was the vocation of Christian men and women to be "as citizens of two cities . . . synthesizing their human, domestic, professional, social, and technical enterprises with religious values."[5]

The people heard these stirring words, and so many more, against a background of a new world reality: unimagined mobility, high technology, instant communication, rapidly changing social mores. As citizens of two cities, the people went beyond the traditional souces of truth, namely the gospel and tradition, and dug into the truth of their experience to discover how best to live in faithful response to the gospel. For the most part their theological, ecclesial, and sociological experiments have been situated in communal contexts: in movements, in parishes and congregations, in small faith communities, in dioceses and judicatories—even in national church bodies.

To some extent, and in some cases, institutional structures are part of the ferment that is breaking open the old categories and creating new possibilities for what the church can be and mean in our time. The people's questions, those that probe and test and stir these old structures, are what I call prophetic. These questions are not conceptualizations; they are lived and living questions. Prophecy belongs to our most ancient traditions. It is, simply stated, the power to break through rigidity and defensiveness to new insights, to a new willingness to change, to new levels of conversion. This power is God's power. We know it is not only found in an individual's words or actions but in the totality of one's life. One is a prophet. There is a familiar shape to Ezekiel or Jeremiah, to John the Baptist, to Dorothy Day or Jean Vanier, to Rufus Jones or John Wesley. They are flesh and blood people, with their own idiosyncrasies and unique expressions of God. And they have made an enormous difference in the life of the church. But from the moment of Pentecost, when the Spirit of God fell like fiery rain upon the earth, Christian prophecy has as often been located in a movement or a social force as in a single, prophetic personality. We need only think of such groups and practices as the sharing, serving communities recorded in Acts, the ordered life of the monastic movement, the Franciscan spirit of simplicity and oneness with all creation, the Reformation's discovery anew of the power of the Word, the Quakers' practice of contemplative waiting and nonviolent behavior, the Methodists' evangelistic preaching, and the populism of American Baptists to see how the overarching church body has been affected by various prophetic movements. The underlying thesis of this book is that prophecy in the church today is concretely occurring around six issues or questions that are profoundly affecting all the Christian churches, reshaping and transfiguring them, and, in the process, strengthening them to engage in the church's major task, the pastoral care of the world. These six prophetic questions are being posed by the laity who are stirring the institutional churches by loyally challenging them. These women and men illustrate what Yves Congar, O.P., meant when he said that the church, if it is to have any meaning for contemporary persons, must be two things. First, it must be a church of transcendence, that is, of teaching the contemplative dimension of religion. Second, it must be a church of human liberation. In other words, it must be both a church for God and a church for humankind.[6]

The six living questions, which I am calling prophetic, are stated here in the form of topics. But at the heart of these "topics" lie energetic questions, questions which press the institutional church to be engaged in these issues to seek deeper understanding, and to be open to new levels of consciousness. The questions are these: (1) *spirituality*, that is, the hunger of ordinary laypeople for direct, experiential knowledge of God as contrasted to knowledge about God; (2) *marriage and family*, including the change from predominantly economic and legalistic arrangements to more personalist and relational ones, and, increasingly, from single-faith to inter-faith marriages; (3) *the changing status and role of women* in society and church and the challenge these bring to the church; (4) *the world of work* as a prime locus for co-creation with God and for evangelization as well; (5) *ministry and mission*, and the new meanings with which the laity are infusing these terms; and (6) *community*, that is, the emergence of small communities of faith and their power to transform society. These six prophetic questions, then, are how I see God's gifted people living out their call to be adult members of the church of Christ, stirring the still waters of the Christian churches, and slowly transfiguring the face of the earth.

One of the most gripping narratives in the Gospel describes in rather fine detail Jesus' transfiguration before his three closest associates.

Peter, James, and John accompany him up a high mountain, away from the curious crowds, away from the Romans, away from the inquiring temple officials, to a place where, Matthew records, "They could be alone" (Matt. 17:1). An unforgettable event happened to Jesus' three companions who saw him utterly changed. "His face shone like the sun and his clothes became white as the light" (Matt. 17:2). There was more. Voices were heard, diverse voices. Moses and Elijah appeared and talked with Jesus. Reality overflowed its banks and touched everything and everyone. "Do not be afraid," Jesus urged, as Peter, James, and John saw him and the whole world differently, at least for the moment.

A. M. Allchin in his classic work on Christian spirituality, *The World Is A Wedding*, expands the image of Jesus' transfiguration to include the transformation of the world. This mountain-top miracle, Allchin insists, released an embracing, salvific, transforming presence throughout the entire world.[7]

What the three apostles saw in Jesus was perfect unity. The cosmic and personal glory of God came forth from the depths of Jesus' being. It was a moment never to be forgotten. And it wasn't. Peter movingly recalls in his Second Letter that unitive moment.

> We had seen his majesty for ourselves. He was honored and glorified by God the Father, when the Sublime Glory itself spoke to him. . . . We heard this ourselves spoken from heaven when we were with him on the holy mountain (2 Pet. 1:16–18)

This remembering of the transfiguration of Jesus is followed by Peter's counsel to Christians that they should depend on prophecy and "take it as a lamp for lighting a way through the dark until the dawn comes and the morning star rises in your minds" (2 Pet. 1:19)—until you recognize yourself as part of this sweeping transfiguration?

Prophecy and transfiguration are the dynamics that draw all life, all men and women, all earth and animals, all sky and planets, all into the oneness of God. And Christians are meant to be part of that process. That's what this book is about: laypeople and the transfiguration of the world; prophetic experiential questions that bring us closer to the unity we Christians long for.

I write as a Catholic, as one who is most in touch with the stirrings within my own church, the church into which I was born and in which I daily seek to exercise the tenets and disciplines of this faith, the Catholic faith. But I write also as a Christian, as one in touch with that wider church and with the diverse streams of religious thought and practice which enliven the broader reality. I write as a citizen of society, a woman who lives in the social, cultural, and civic contexts of life as well as in the church sanctuaries and meeting halls. These six questions are mine, but they belong to the laity of other Christian traditions as well. I know this to be so because the questions are there when we meet in the different secular and church arenas that bring laity of many different churches together. And as we struggle to live these questions, we are helping each other to stay with the light, the revealing and energizing light that continues to pour from the holy mountain, from the holy world, that illuminates the kingdom of God, little by little.

One of the assumptions underlying this book is that the world is a good and holy place. It is, after all, God's world. And it follows that the ordinary daily activities of men and women in the world share in what Richard Mouw calls a holy worldliness.[8] The structure of the book follows this assumption. Each chapter opens with a few lines from a secular work: a novel, a poem, an essay not explicitly in the religious genre—at least you wouldn't be able to locate the work under that category in the library's card catalogue. This choice is partly to draw attention to the need for uncovering religious reality in the language of the world, and partly to point to the need for fresh, contemporary images to reflect God's ceaseless action on our behalf. And each chapter closes with some suggestions for further study and reflection. While these books, articles, and publications are in no sense exhaustive, they do provide the reader with additional resources, filling in the gaps and amplifying certain issues embedded in the prophetic questions discussed in this book.

NOTES

1. "Decree on Ecumenism," in Walter M. Abbott, S. J., ed., *The Documents of Vatican II*, no. 1 (New York: Herder & Herder/Associated Press, 1966), 341.
2. "Gaudium et Spes," in *The Documents of Vatican II*, no. 49, 252–53.
3. "Gaudium et Spes," in *The Documents of Vatican II*, no. 29, 227–28.

4. "Lumen Gentium," in *The Documents of Vatican II*, no. 40, 67.

5. "Gaudium et Spes," in *The Documents of Vatican II*, no. 43, 242–43.

6. Yves Congar, in an address delivered at a European meeting of Catholic bishops on the topic of the bishops' pastoral responsibility for the lay apostolate. The meeting was held in Vienna in July 1981. Proceedings of this conference are available from the Pontifical Council for the Laity, Vatican City, Europe.

7. A. M. Allchin, *The World Is a Wedding* (New York: Oxford Univ. Press, 1978).

8. Richard J. Mouw, *Called to Holy Worldliness* (Philadelphia: Fortress Press, 1980).

1

Spirituality

> One day when I was sitting quiet and feeling like a mother-
> less child, which I was, it come to me: that feeling of being
> part of everything, not separate at all. I knew that if I cut a
> tree, my arm would bleed. And I laughed and I cried and I
> run all round the house. I knew just what it was. In fact when
> it happen you can't miss it.
>
> Shug Avery in Alice Walker, *The Color Purple*

SHUG AVERY, a poor black woman in Alice Walker's novel about the
deep South in the first decades of this century, is a natural contemplative. God is in the air she breathes, and she knows it. She belongs to
the universe, and it belongs to her. Between the woman and the world
there exists a tender intimacy.

Shug's experience is similar to that of contemplative personalities
across time and culture who in their openness to the transcendent
permit a shattering of ego boundaries. This "dying" yields fresh vision,
understanding, a sense of belonging and abiding peace. This transcendent vision comes at different points along the way. Characterized by
open searching it has often been referred to by Christians as spiritual
pilgrimage. Along its route one falls into the knowledge of God—not
knowledge *about* God so much as knowledge *of* God—simple knowing.
But the phrase falling into knowing is not quite accurate. It is more like
growing into knowing, although it may feel like falling, as it did for
Shug when she raced about laughing and crying at the wonder of its
simplicity.

This coinherence of all life in God has been described by saints and mystics of both Catholic and Protestant traditions. One thinks of Saint Francis and his sense of intimacy with the birds and the animals as well as with his free-spirited band of spiritual brothers, the mendicants, or of Dame Julian of Norwich who so unself-consciously reverenced the earth and all it holds. The image of her cradling a small hazelnut in her hand and seeing in it the greatness and majesty of God is one imprinted on Western spiritual consciousness. And like Jacob Boehme with his recognition of God in the shaft of light reflected from a common pewter dish and George Fox with his indefatigable following of the inner light, there are so many more who have seen in and through the ordinary environment to the One who creates and sustains, the One "in whom we live and move and have our being" (Acts 17:28).

Francis of Assisi and Dame Julian, Jacob Boehme and George Fox—all were laypeople whose lives and teaching were marked by prophetic spiritual insights powerful enough to move fellow pilgrims toward new levels of inner freedom and outward responsibility. The same can be said for laymen and laywomen of our own time. I speak of ordinary people who, like their Christian ancestors, are spiritual pilgrims forging new pathways. And what are some of these pathways?

Spiritual Movements

Consider this scene. In a retreat house in the suburbs approximately thirty-five men, seated at round tables in groups of seven, are listening intently to a speaker. He's talking to them about Christian action, but not in the abstract. He's telling them about his life, about people who have loved him into believing that he is precious to God, infinitely precious. He's telling them about his wife, his children, his work. He's trying to explain in earthy language who Christ is to him and how he experiences his relationship with Christ. The room is bristling with emotion. He is one of many speakers throughout a long weekend. After each talk, the listeners speak to one another in the trusted atmosphere of their small table groups. Gradually, as the weekend unfolds, their talk expresses the secrets of their hearts as well as their minds. During the days together, these men will pray with each other, both aloud and in the solitude of silence. Most probably, they will cry with each other too and wonder at their tears. Mail from the outside world will arrive at their secluded retreat, and they will learn that men and women who themselves have experienced a similar weekend are praying for them, fasting for them, and performing a variety of sacrifices so that these men may be open to the action of the Holy Spirit. This is a Cursillo weekend. At its conclusion the men will be welcomed in a most festive way into the larger Cursillo community. They will be supported by the movement in their individual and corporate mission to transform the environment of society into a community of grace. Another weekend will see a similar scenario, only the participants will be women.

The spirit of the Cursillo movement, that is, prayer, study, and action in the context of Christian community for the purpose of transforming the societal environment into places of love and justice, is kept alive through regular small-group meetings. These consist of four or five persons at most. The meeting is called the reunion of friends. Spanish in origin, the Cursillo movement has adapted remarkably well to the busy, productive, achievement-conscious American lifestyle. And, while initially designed by Catholics, the movement is now alive in some Protestant denominations as well.

While the weekend will typically have ordained and lay members on the presenting team and among the "candidates" for admission, the leadership and the membership of the Cursillo movement are predominantly lay. It is a movement that is growing across all kinds of boundaries—national and church, race and class—bonding Christian laypeople together at the level of spirit. While Cursillo members often invite fellow parishioners to become part of the movement, it is clearly a transparochial movement.

Imagine another scene: the basement of a Methodist church in a small-sized city. It is Wednesday evening. Men and women of all ages are gathered in several concentric circles. Many have Bibles in their hands or on their laps. All seem deep in prayer. In some cases arms are lifted upward, reaching to the heavens. Some Scripture is read and there is praying aloud, all spontaneously. After a while a great collective voice rises in a chant-like song of syllables, sounds, and words— clearly not English. This is a charismatic prayer group, and they are "singing in tongues."

Well, you say, Pentecostal groups have been around for quite some time. True. What is different about this group is that the members, by

and large, worship regularly in this particular Methodist church, not
with the local Assembly of God. Furthermore, this kind of charismatic
gathering could just as likely take place in Our Lady of Lourdes Catholic Church or in Faith Lutheran Church. Charismatic prayer, or the
renewal as many prefer to call the phenomenon, is a spiritual movement
on fire in many denominations. And, in many cases, the pray-ers freely
cross denominational lines to be together to praise God in a free, unin-
hibited way. Again, while clergy are certainly part of this movement,
its broad-based leadership is largely lay.

Charismatics number in the hundreds of thousands, and they are all
over the world. While carefully constructed and monitored dialogues
continue responsibly to illuminate the theological questions of our
denominational commonality and difference, the joyful, exuberant
experience of charismatic prayer has moved ecumenical relationships
to a spiritual center, at least in the everyday life of ordinary people.[1]

These are but two examples of spiritual movements, of people gathered in a somewhat organized way and with clarity of purpose, seeking
God in the company of one another, as pilgrims of every age have done.
There are, however, other faces of spirituality in the Christian
churches.

Prayer of the East

When I was growing up in New York City, in an Irish Catholic ghetto
of sorts, other Christians were distant, even suspect. I house a vivid
memory of standing across the street from a Protestant church (I was
about six years old) in the company of my small friend. We were waiting to glimpse her Sunday school teacher dressed in her beautiful bridal
clothes as she entered the church for her wedding. I stood there under
a cloud of guilt, a betrayer to my own kind, the Catholic kind. I think
I must have confessed this at the time of my first confession, although
I have no clear recollection of that. I know I unburdened my conscience
to my mother—a rather daring act, since she did not favor different
others. I had no inkling on that long ago day that my journey of soul
and spirit would be so encouraged, nurtured, and strengthened by the
insights of Protestants as it has been; nor had I any glimpse that I would
learn much from the great religious traditions of the East.

Years ago I read in one of Thomas Merton's articles or books that the new ecumenical frontier was appearing in the East. He meant, of course, that significant movement toward spiritual liberation would come from the exchange between Christians, who were seekers and could see something of value in Eastern practice, and members of the Eastern religious traditions, who recognized the spiritual heart of the Christian way. It took the dissatisfaction of the youth culture of the sixties to bring Eastern prayer practices into the spiritual lives of ordinary Christian men and women. Merton was a herald. If he, who was guiding the spiritual journey of so many (often unknowingly), looked to the East for inner knowledge, then perhaps the "guided" could drink at that well too. And so, Christian meditation groups learned that chanting aloud could calm both body and mind and open the human heart to sacred stillness. Christians seemed to learn from the East a new reverence for the body as a true temple of the Holy Spirit. This meant that it was not only "all right" but really important to pay attention to muscles, which often hold so much tension, reflecting our tenseness vis-à-vis God, and to posture, which directs our attention to the silent, present moment. Stretching the body, massaging away the tenseness, straightening the back, assuming a relaxed but alert position for prayer, breathing correctly and using sound to still the mind were found to be helpful preparation for open, contemplative prayer. Sitting, so central to the practice of Zen, introduced laity and clergy alike to simply waiting upon God.

The Shalem Institute for Spiritual Formation is one of the pioneers in the wedding of East and West in the search for union with God. Visit a Shalem meditation group and you will witness twenty or so men and women, Protestant and Catholic, clergy, lay, and vowed religious, sitting in silence. Some lean against the wall of the meditation room; some are in the classic lotus position. They will have started their two-hour early morning or early evening meditation period with body exercise and with some kind of Christian chant. Perhaps "Kyrie Eleison," Greek for "Lord have mercy," will be used to lead them into the silence. There will also be some sharing with spiritual friends within the group and perhaps input from the group leader.

Meditation groups are central to Shalem's corporate life. They marked Shalem's beginnings over ten years ago. But since that time, the vision and commitment have expanded to include the sponsorship of national conferences on spirituality, contractual work with parishes and congregations, and two national programs for training spiritual directors.

While Shalem is explicitly focused on Christian spirituality, it is clearly shaped by the director Rev. Tilden Edwards's long experience with religious social concerns, which in any major urban center must be broadly ecumenical. Shalem consciously connects the spiritual journey with care for the social order, and it does so with respect for a variety of religious expressions, including the contributions of the East.

In Shalem settings Quakers and Congregationalists, Episcopalians and Catholics, Lutherans and Presbyterians find in their shared silence and their shared ministry for the world a knitting of many spirits. The Shalem pilgrims discover how much of value they truly share and how much they can learn from non-Christian religions. This is a reminder that God is the God of all.[2]

Spiritual Direction

One of the most respected and ancient ministries of the church is that of spiritual direction. In both Western and Eastern Christianity, the wise and holy man or woman willing to seek with others the leadings of the Holy Spirit has been a source of nourishment to hungry souls. The desert fathers in Egypt, Syria, and Palestine—and the desert mothers as well[3]—provide us with the first records of this particular form of Christian companionship. Those practiced in prayer and virtue and knowing the intricacies of the human ego taught others who sought God with sincere hearts what they themselves had learned through hard-fought interior struggles.

Spiritual direction moved with Christian spirituality from the desert into the monasteries, and also into the laity's life outside the monastery walls. During the Middle Ages groups of penitents gave and received spiritual counsel, and in the twelfth century books and manuals of lay direction appeared.[4] Ignatius of Loyola, Francis de Sales, Teresa of Jesus, and John of the Cross are names most frequently associated with spiritual direction within the Catholic tradition. And within Anglicanism, George Herbert, Augustine Baker, Jeremy Taylor, Evelyn Underhill, and Martin Thornton are frequently mentioned as enriching the Christian understanding and practice of spiritual guidance. Kenneth

Leech points out that within Reformation Protestantism there also is precedent for the exercise of this particular charism. While clearly opposed to the need for mediation between the soul and God, such illustrious leaders as Luther and Zwingli recognized the peace of mind that can grow from consultation with another Christian learned in the ways of the soul. Although the Quakers stressed guidance from within the human person, George Fox was, in fact, a spiritual guide.[5] And in our generation Dietrich Bonhoeffer, a Lutheran pastor, and Thomas Kelly and Douglas Steere, both Quakers, have served through their writings as spiritual guides of post–World War II Christians.

Twenty years ago my family of four very young children, my husband, and myself attended our first family retreat. During the course of our weekend with other Catholic families the subject of spiritual direction was introduced into the group discussions. One couple, parents of nine children, spoke of the benefits to them as individuals and as a couple of meeting regularly with a priest to, in the language of the sixties, "process their inner lives." As a teenager I had experienced spiritual direction, chiefly during a period of discernment about my vocation. Again, in the period prior to my marriage, I had met regularly with a priest, probing the implications of the step I was about to take. My husband-to-be also took counsel with this priest, and sometimes we three met together, a rather unusual practice for Catholics in the fifties. During the course of this particular family retreat, I recalled how supported and stretched I had felt because of this special spiritual relationship and realized that since my marriage and the responsibilities of parenthood, I had felt "too busy" to seek spiritual counsel. Now I saw it was possible for someone like me, immersed in active family and civic life, to have a spiritual director. That was the beginning.

Many years later I recognize this sacred space and time as an important opportunity for my hastening along on the spiritual journey. I have found that spiritual direction is a place where the original, essential self is evoked, where I realize more fully who I am before God. Certainly it is not the only place. Marriage and family life are in themselves revelatory of God. So are friendship, work, and ministry. But spiritual direction affords windows onto all these other experiences of growth in God.

Until recently my experience could not have been regarded as typical. For a long time spiritual direction was thought to be "a Catholic thing," and then available only to monks and nuns—a resource for those thought to be far advanced in prayer and spiritual maturity. And among Catholics there was resistance to a one-to-one relationship in which there was thought to be a relinquishment of personal authority; renewal within the Catholic church eschewed authoritarianism in any form. But the renaissance within the Catholic church is yielding a reclamation of this vital ministry. Not only are laypeople seeking wise and holy counsel, they too are discovering that some in their number are especially graced to be spiritual directors. Furthermore, they are seeking training in order faithfully to respond to their call.

And, it must be said, that spiritual direction is no longer "the Catholic thing." Anglicans and Reformation Protestants sense significant personal and corporate spiritual gain in this intentional journeying together. Ann Ulanov, Episcopalian psychotherapist and spiritual director, maintains that people are needful of safe, unhurried places where they may deal with their inner images. These images constitute the primary language of the psyche or soul, and as such they are charged with energy and creative possibilities. The boredom that many associate with church, Ulanov claims, is due to the church's failure to help people get in touch with their own images. The result is that many traditional biblical images are devoid of meaning for vast numbers of churchgoers, and most nonchurchgoers. Spiritual direction is one place of encounter that Ulanov suggests might remedy the image-emptiness of so many of our churches. Of course, for our churches to be places of spiritual discovery and counsel, there must be the willingness to allow people— pastoral leadership as well as ordinary men and women—to "waste time," to be together for the long haul, not simply for short-term problem-solving as is the case with so much pastoral counseling. It seems that people sense that good spiritual resources help them to deal with stress, a common ailment of contemporary life. Prayer and spiritual direction are recognized as enabling people to live a good, human life, a perception that is genuinely incarnational.

Scripture Study

The late Urban Holmes, dean of the department of theology at The University of the South, once said that what was needed for spiritual renewal was an evangelization of the mind. The surge of Scripture study among the laity is one mark, I believe, of such an evangelization. During the last twenty-five years our churches have been places of rich encounter between the people and the Word of God. This has been happening both formally and informally.

Perhaps this sign of spiritual vitality is most notable in the Catholic church where until the Second Vatican Council laypeople, by and large, kept a safe distance from the Scriptures. But with the council's emphasis on the priesthood of all believers and the invitation to "let the treasure of revelation entrusted to the church increasingly fill the hearts of men"[6] the laity began to explore the interesting terrain of biblical literature. They did so intellectually, but more important, they also did so with the heart—spiritually. Today it is not uncommon to find laypeople enrolled in Scripture courses in colleges, seminaries, or adult theological centers, and engaged in formal study. But perhaps even more striking is the number of laymen and laywomen who meet in small groups under parish auspices to study the Scriptures in order to apply the wisdom of God to their personal lives and to the common life of the communities where they live and work. In this way Catholics are sharing yet another link with Protestant laity who have for many years found strength, insight, and inner freedom through Scripture study.

The Arts

Madeleine L'Engle writes that "the widow's mite and Bach's St. Matthew's Passion are both living mysteries, both witness to lives which affirm the loving presence of God."[7] What she means, of course, is that Christian life and health are nourished not only by the Scriptures (or sacraments, or rituals, or spiritual guidance, or all the obvious "spiritual means") but also by the beauty of human imagination. The arts as pathways of spiritual development are increasingly a part of every serious discussion of Christian spirituality: a new language is being articulated, one with new categories and formulations. Dancers and sculptors, novelists and poets, musicians and painters are the crafters of the fresh symbols that speak of the unspeakable Mystery. Actually, this is not so terribly new. Dante and George Herbert, Fra Angelico and Rubens, Beethoven and countless other artists have for centuries revealed the mysterious beauty of God.

Several years ago I interviewed a singer and pianist, Isabella Bates, who with her musician husband, Steven, and their two children lives and works in Washington, D.C., gleaning her story of equality in marriage for inclusion in a book I was working on.[8] Several blessings flowed from that interview. One was an inspiring and honest story for my book. The other was the ignition of a quiet flame within me: the desire to resume my own study of piano.

For some time I had known that I was in need of a nonverbal route for my continuing inner growth. Words—writing, reading, speaking— form the social fabric of my professional ministerial life, and even the small contribution I make to parish life as a Sunday lector involves words. Wordless prayer was part of my devotional life—but was it really so wordless? I had had a dream about weaving, complete with a master plan for converting my screened porch into an enclosed weaver's studio. Was I romanticizing? Perhaps, but I did more than dream; I embarked on a strategy for moving toward my goal. Being a cautious person, I started small: weekly crochet lessons. Get the feel of working with yarn, I said, and before long you can move on to the weaver's loom. I supplied myself with beautiful yarns and patterns for hats (which I love), crochet hooks, and promises to my friends that from now on their gifts from me would be handmade. I was a faithful student. And I was miserable. What I hadn't realized was that not having acquired handwork skills in my youth would slow my learning. My classmates in the beginners' group all had some past experience with the craft. I was confused and discouraged. One day I looked at my piano, then tucked away in the corner of the basement recreation room.

I had been a student of piano from age six to eighteen, but when I left high school for college I left my music behind, along with my school uniform. True, when I married, my husband transported my childhood piano to our new home several states away. It remained part of my environment, reminding me to teach Christmas carols to the children and to see to their piano lessons. But for so long now I had ignored what this patient instrument of beauty had to offer. I called Isabella and asked if she would take me as a pupil.

That was over two years ago. What am I learning? Certainly I'm discovering the measured and intricate balance of Bach, the rich melody of Schubert, the fun of Mozart. But more, I am learning about myself and how I address myself to life. I see now that I approach a piece of music as I do everything else: with a fierce determination to finish quickly in a somewhat acceptable fashion. Isabella insists that I slow down and reach down into one or two measures. When I try this, that is, when I am docile or teachable, and actually do what she asks, I find moments of communion and fulfillment: I am at one with the music. I have given some thought as to why my return to the piano has been so satisfying and my foray into the world of textiles so frustrating, and I have concluded that in midlife recalling a previously learned skill can move one from the level of technique to art.

Robert McGovern is an artist whose principal medium is woodcut. His subjects are religious figures, and his spirit concretized in his work transcends any particular denomination. Twenty some years ago I bought two of his works. Having little money and being untutored in the proper framing of such art I enclosed them in department store frames. For a few years they were in the public rooms of my home. Then one, Mary of Nazareth, went to my office. The other, the Sacred Heart, retired to a cupboard in the basement. A visit to Ireland jarred my ancestral memory as I saw, in one Irish kitchen after another, representations of the Sacred Heart, a peculiarly Catholic devotion. I came home from Ireland and brought my McGovern Sacred Heart to our local framing shop. There everyone exclaimed over its likeness to Picasso. We framed it in oak, and it hung in the shop window for a month while passers-by inquired after the artist and the subject. A year later I met Robert McGovern at a conference sponsored by my office. I saw that his lower body is paralyzed. I saw too the strength of his spirit, which neither polio nor I expect anything else can constrict. After the conference he wrote these words:

> I desire that all participate with me in my forming art. All of this so that the uncarved blocks of the future will be shaped with a mutual strength. The faith we hold brings us to a radiant strength that emanates from Christ . . . a constellation in Himself to which we gather, possessed of a light too great for us to measure. Yet art is such that I strive to meet it. . . .[9]

As pastors and theologians seek to express the richness of Christian faith to late twentieth-century Christians and non-Christians, they might do well to explore the intuitive, artistic way of knowing, seeking insight from dance and film, music and literature, the fine arts, pottery, and, yes, weaving. It would seem that a new kind of seeing and a fresh kind of praise is in order.

The Scientific Quest

When one reads the work of scientists such as Albert Einstein or Stephen Hawking, one touches the holiness in their uncompromising search for the secrets of the universe. Their search for the truth shares in the purity of single-mindedness, that quality which the gospel says cleanses the vision so that God may be seen. Theologians are now studying physicists for clues to ultimate meaning and to the nature and purpose of God's creative and sustaining life. John Haught is one such theologian. A professor at Georgetown University in Washington, D.C., Dr. Haught's book, *The Cosmic Adventure*,[10] probes the value of our individual lives against the backdrop of scientific discovery and speculation. He contends that in the broadest sense religion is not opposed to science and that science can be revealing of the spiritual dimensions of life.

> I wrote *The Cosmic Adventure* because I have encountered a spiritual hunger among some of the students and other intelligent people who are scientifically informed. They want some vision of the universe in which they can feel their lives are ultimately significant. Their problem is that in reading scientific journals—and popular presentations of science such as those by Robert Jastrow, Carl Sagan and Isaac Asimov—they have come to believe that science rules out a purposeful interpretation of the cosmos.[11]

Haught believes, however, that science, undertaken humbly, can lead to a sense of awe at the depth of the cosmos as profound as that of any religious seer.

This has been the experience of the physicist Fritjof Capra who believes that modern physics is leading us to a view of the world that is very similar to the views held by mystics of all ages and traditions. Capra writes of transcending opposites. He speaks of force and matter, particles and waves, motion and rest, existence and nonexistence as some of the opposite or contradictory concepts which are transcended in modern physics.[12] It is precisely this embracing of opposites that the theologian Haught identifies with Jesus Christ.

> In the story of Jesus the Christian is attracted to the expansiveness of the

man from Nazareth who reaches out in the broadest possible way in order to integrate into his life the widest variety of people and experiences. The story pictures Jesus as embracing tax collectors, prostitutes, rich and poor, the socially respected and the socially rejected, women as well as men, children and adults, heretics along with the orthodox, the sick and the healthy.[13]

Many agree with the geneticist Dr. Edmond Murphy who points out that we live in an age in which the major cultural factor is science. He therefore argues for dialogue among theologians, pastoral leadership, and scientists, saying "Some problems are so radically new that the whole solution, morals and all, must be built up from scratch. The ideal way is by a communion of minds."[14]

What are the experiences of scientists? What metaphors of God do they have for us? How can we dip into their discoveries? How can the churches broker a new dialogue between science and religion, one that is respectful of the truth that abides with each? These are some of the questions that thoughtful laity are raising among themselves.

Summary

The contemporary pathways of spiritual development discussed above—movements, Eastern prayer-ways, spiritual guidance and direction, renewed Scripture study, the arts, and the scientific quest for truth—are filled with men, women, and children from many different religious traditions. Like pilgrims of old they discover in their extra-parochial journey together something new and precious, a gospel pearl perhaps. Like missionaries, they bring to their at-home congregations a new consciousness, because they cannot forget what they have seen, and heard, and what they now know. Their presence questions the status quo, and over time their presence can transform the face of the church. How?

> You know how it is. You ast yourself one question, it lead to fifteen. . . . I think us here to wonder, to ast. And that in wondering bout the big things and asting bout the big things, you learn about the little ones, almost by accident. But you never know nothing more about the big things than you start out with. The more I wonder, he say, the more I love.[15]

So speaks Albert, a character in *The Color Purple*.

The spiritual quest has always promised the great paradox of inner freedom and deep bonding with others. Today's laity partakes in both the tradition and the quest, and this brings to the churches a gentle challenge to pause and to take stock of their spiritual treasures.

NOTES

1. The National Conference of Catholic Bishops has recently published a pastoral statement on the charismatic renewal. It is available from the USCC Office of Publishing and Promotion Services, Washington, D.C.
2. Shalem sponsors a number of spiritual development programs, including retreats, workshops, quiet days, conferences, meditation groups, and local and residential programs in spiritual direction. Information may be obtained by writing to Shalem, Mt. St. Alban, Washington, D.C. 20016.
3. See Benedicta Ward, *Sayings of the Desert Fathers* (Kalamazoo, Mich.: Cistercian Publications, 1975), who identifies four desert mothers and their particular wisdom.
4. Kenneth Leech, *Soul Friend* (London: Sheldon Press, 1977), provides a succinct but thorough historical context for the ministry of spiritual direction.
5. Ibid., 84–88.
6. "Dogmatic Constitution on Revelation," in *Documents of Vatican II*, no. 26, 128. This document emphasized that Catholics understand the source of revelation to be both Scripture and tradition.
7. Madeleine L'Engle, *Walking on Water: Reflections on Faith and Art* (New York: Bantam Books, 1982), 31.
8. Dolores Leckey, *The Ordinary Way: A Family Spirituality* (New York: Crossroad Pub. Co., 1982).
9. Robert McGovern, "Wordless Art," *New Catholic World* (May/June 1984).
10. John Haught, *The Cosmic Adventure: Science, Religion and the Quest for Purpose.* (Ramsey, N.J.: Paulist Press, 1984).
11. Brad Lemly, an interview with John Haught, *Washington Post Magazine* 7 October 1984.
12. Fritjof Capra, *The Tao of Physics* (New York: Bantam Books, 1980).
13. John Haught, in Lemly, interview.
14. Edmond Murphy, *New Catholic World* (May/June 1984).
15. Alice Walker, *The Color Purple* (New York: Harcourt Brace Jovanovich, 1982), 239.

FOR FURTHER READING

de Waal, Esther. *Seeking God.* Collegeville, Minn.: The Liturgical Press, 1984.
Edwards, Tilden. *Spiritual Friendship.* Mahwah, N.J.: Paulist Press, 1980.
Green, Thomas, S. J. *Darkness in the Marketplace: The Christian at Prayer in the World.* Notre Dame, Ind.: Ave Maria Press, 1981.

Kelsey, Morton. *Encounter With God.* London: Hodder & Stoughton, 1974.
May, Gerald. *Will and Spirit.* San Francisco: Harper & Row, 1982.
The Classics of Western Spirituality, A Library of Great Spiritual Masters. Mahwah, N.J.: Paulist Press. This is a series of new translations and studies of Western mystics, both Catholic and Protestant.
The Tree of Hope. This publication contains the proceedings of a national conference held in 1982 on American spirituality and its relationship to social justice, and is available from the Office of Publishing and Promotion Services, United States Catholic Conference, Washington D.C.

2

Marriage and Family: The Domestic Church

Love alters not with his brief hours and weeks,
But bears it out even to the edge of doom.
                              William Shakespeare, Sonnet 116

MOST LAY PEOPLE will name their families as their primary context for spiritual life, formation, and development. The biblical metaphor of marriage as God's relationship with humankind is still surprisingly apt. If we want to know how and what God is communicating, look at marriage and family.

Until recently men and women married, had children, and grew old together loving, or at least bearing it out even to the edge of doom. If they were religious people likely they belonged to the same religious faith. Familial roles were fairly well-defined. Men worked outside the home and provided the material sustenance for the family. Women were homemakers. A strong sense of duty prevailed that focused on raising children, with love growing stronger as duty did.

But the glue in the institution of marriage was fundamentally legal and biological. For example, until the Second Vatican Council the Catholic church's primary view of marriage was as both a contract, and as the vehicle for the procreation and education of children. I suspect the same was true in other Christian traditions.

Much of that has changed—for everyone. The movement of women from the expected and church-approved homemaker role into professional and public roles is now a reality. (The profound changes in the lives of women and the impact of this on the churches are discussed in the following chapter.) Divorce, a fact of modern life, is now as wide-spread among Christians as it is in the overall population. Single par-ents are to be found in any given congregation—at least those who have not given up on the church. Ecumenical or interfaith marriage, or mar-riage with a non-believer, is not the rarity it once was; in fact, it is closer to the norm. What underlies these major shifts in practice? And what is to be learned from these signs of the times?

I think one common factor related to all the changes mentioned is the personalist expectations that people now bring to their marriages. Everyone expects to grow in the relationship, to experience the qualities associated with the kingdom of God, namely, peace, righteousness, freedom, and justice. Another factor is a new openness in Christian theology, evidenced by a stance of dialogue with other disciplines. At its best, this dynamism emphasizes the worth and dignity of every human person.

One of the most significant dialogues is that between psychology and theology. The various psychological disciplines have made Western Christians aware of the possibilities for human potential and growth. Theology admittedly is enriched by such dialogue, and now many psy-chiatrists and psychologists admit to the benefits received from the ordered, systematic theological reflection and spiritual wisdom that are the Church's heritage.[1] What psychology and psychoanalysis have helped people of the church to see is that underneath our social roles, duties, and obligations, there exists a locus of desire and longing, an impetus to personal change and to becoming. Of course, spiritual direc-tors and counselors, good ones that is, historically have uncovered the same thing: the spiritual core, the self, the person. This new dialogue has signaled a movement away from the idea of marriage as solely a social and religious contract to the experience of marriage as a meeting of persons who grow in love with one another, mutually influencing one another in a reciprocal sharing of power. It is a movement from contract to covenant. This personalist/relational theology was recently expressed by Pope John Paul II in his apostolic letter, "To the Youth of the World." Speaking about the different aspects of the laity's voca-tion, he says, "To set out on the path of the married vocation means to learn married love day by day, year by year: love according to soul and body, love that is 'patient, is kind, that does not insist on its own way . . . and does not rejoice at wrong . . . love that rejoices in the right, love that endures all things.' " [1 Cor. 13:4-7]. The pope continues, "It is precisely this love that you young people need if your married future is to 'pass the test' of the whole of life. And precisely this test is part of the very essence of the vocation which, through marriage, you intend to include in the plan of life. . . ."[2]

Jack Dominian, English psychiatrist and frequent contributor to religious journals and books, is a steady partner in the personalist/relational dialogue. His research and reflection suggest to him that the key to the life of the family is not the children but the relationship of the couple. "Marriage is primarily about the life of the couple from whose love everything else emanates."[3] Dominian describes this deeply personal marital love as sustaining, healing, and growthful. Emotional support is central, allowing movement toward a center of intimacy wherein the couple can open to each other their deepest inner wounds and then receive healing. The healing doesn't occur automatically but involves action: acknowledgment of deprivation, perhaps; alteration of some fear or bad habit; or some other change. Growth proceeds over time, enabling the couple to show affection, control emotions of anger and irritation, acquire tolerance, understanding, and forgiveness. These dynamics, Dominian asserts, open one to marriage as a sacramental reality, a graced covenant,[4] a vehicle for moving from hardened privatistic individualism to becoming a "we," a community of life and love. There is in this vision some glimmer of awareness that in its ebb and flow life together is the place of encounter with Christ. One experiences in the other, the spouse, the possibility of the light bearer, "of bringing to light all that is hidden" (Luke 8:17), of illuminating within us the dark, cobwebby corners we'd rather not poke around in. In this daily lived covenant with another there is the hope of salvation and of abundant life. And so, the routines of shopping and meals, cleaning and gardening, the ordinary talk, the ordinary fights, the giving and receiving of affection, the hurts that heal, and even those that smolder, the moments of sexual intimacy—all these can reflect the ultimate, loving presence of God. In marriage we have the gift of serving as icons for each other, seeing through to that abiding love which is richer beyond all imagination. Of course, the converse is also true. We can, and often do, disfigure the image of God within us or dishonor it in the other.

The point of all of this is to situate the sacrament of marriage in the truest context, namely the daily lived experience of the man and the woman who at one time publicly expressed their intent, before a gathering of the church, to remain in intimate relationship with each other forever. Too often, the ritual has been thought of as the sacrament when it is only the beginning, the first step in an unknown, adventuresome sacramental journey together.

Most theologians working in the area of marriage agree with their colleagues in the psychological profession that sexuality is a principal means of communication between husband and wife. Yet, Christianity is unique among world religions in its nonrecognition of the value of the erotic in human life and growth.[5] That's why Dr. Dominian's reflections on the meaning of sexual expression in marriage are so welcome. He writes, "Intercourse is a body language in which the erotic becomes the channel of communication for personal love."[6] How is love communicated?

First, the sexual experience is saturated with pleasure and joy and in the course of making love the couple are thanking each other. They may do this with or without words.

Second, the act, a source of immense pleasure, calls for repetition. This may be immediately, soon, the next day, the day after or as soon as possible. Implicit in this repetition is the hope of being responded to and wanted. This mutual trust is constantly reinforced. From childhood, we hope that we are loved; we build that hope through adulthood.

Third, the couple will have conflicts and hurt each other. There will be mutual forgiveness, but some hurt will remain. In the depth of intercourse there will be found a powerful joy which will wipe away the hurt. So this is an act of forgiveness and reconciliation.

Fourth, intercourse most economically confirms the sexual identity of each other. The man is able to make his wife feel most completely a woman and the wife able to make her husband feel most completely a man. Thus this is the recurrent way in which the couple confirm the divine image in each other as sexual beings.

Fifth, from the very beginning of life we depend on the sense of our personhood being affirmed by those who love us. Every time a couple make love, they indicate to each other that they recognize, want and appreciate the other. Intercourse is therefore a recurrent affirmation of each other. . . .

All this can be summed up by saying that every sexual act gives life to the couple and on one or two occasions it gives new life.[7]

Thankfulness, trust, forgiveness and reconciliation, sexual identity and the divine image, personal affirmation—if these are the sexual dynamics of marriage (communicated not only through intercourse, but through the many details of sexual presence to one another, day after day), they are also religious dynamics, and concretely Christian. Dr. David Thomas, one of the leading theologians in the field of marriage and family life, would, I believe, support the Dominian position. Dr. Thomas insists that within the human interactions of marriage, enriched and empowered by God, is found what might appear to be impossible to the skeptic or nonbeliever, namely, genuine love.[8]

These insights into marital intimacy and growth in the spirit are not strictly "denominational," applicable to one particular Christian group or another. They cut across all traditions. The issue is how to make them alive in real marriages, which more often than not are and will be ecumenical marriages. There is a growing urgency here when we consider divorce, always traumatic for spouses and children, and the fact of rising divorce statistics, a fact affecting all churches. Even the most sympathetic sociologists of religion refer to divorce as a leading social evil of our day. They advocate fighting it not in a negative way but pastorally, and by recognizing that the divorced are often seeking a greater expression of love in their lives. The all-too-present possibility of divorce presents a reasonable challenge to the churches: that of adequate preparation for marriage and family life. Equally important is the necessity of providing concrete support after marriage, particularly in various life transitions which are in themselves stressful and which consequently increase the stress in the marital relationship. What can be done?

Marriage Preparation and Marriage Enrichment

Several years ago I attended a national-level Roman Catholic/Episcopalian dialogue. The informal dialogue was as revealing to me as the formal, official sessions. One day during lunch an Episcopalian priest and I discovered we had arrived at some common hopes for our children, all of whom were young adults. We agreed that at the very least we hoped our children would marry believers, believers in something that stood as a counterforce to so much free-floating nihilism. Then, one notch above simple belief, we acknowledged it would be a good thing if our children chose as spouses men and women who had been raised in the Christian tradition, and who were still practicing Christians. Finally, we allowed that there would probably be fewer external and internal obstacles to overcome if our offspring married within their own particular expression of Christian faith: Roman Catholic or Episcopalian. In all honesty we thought it unlikely that the third scenario would unfold for all our children (eight between us). A more likely marital alliance, we thought, was the first or second situation.

I think our conversation reflected some general concerns among believing Christians. As we worry about and pray for our growing and grown children it seems important to live in realistic hope. Ecumenical marriages are of a piece with this realism, and together, in collaboration, the Christian churches can point us toward hope.

In many places throughout the United States common guidelines for ecumenical marriages are enabling creative steps in marriage preparation. These guidelines recommend joint premarital counseling wherever possible and spell out individual responsibilities. They also identify areas that need special attention: respect for both religious traditions, patterns of joint and separate worship, responsible parenthood, religious education of the children, and the common understanding of marriage as sacramental.

As important as these elements are, one cannot help but wonder if the premarital instructions also include some indication of the importance of sexual communication for the health of the marriage, as well as common agreement about issues of parenting, spiritual and emotional growth in marriage, psychological readiness for marriage, the centrality of friendship and mutual respect, and the personal resources needed for commitment for life. In addition to doctrinal clarification, marriage preparation should point to the human and spiritual elements of a healthy and life-giving marriage. A realistic hope is that the local church will suggest and offer to couples concrete supports for their marital journey and for the life of their domestic church. On the other hand, the experience of family has something to say to the wider church. In particular, interfaith families may have a prophetic word that deserves to be listened to with respect.

Consider Walt and Anita who have been married for sixteen years.

Anita is a practicing Episcopalian, Walt a practicing Catholic. When they met and dated, their religious affiliations were as important to them as they are now. During their courtship, conversations about marriage inevitably turned toward children. If they were to marry, how could they raise their children in such a way as to be respectful of both their traditions? In some ways, they say, Walt's Catholicism was dominant in the premarital years and in the early years of their marriage. Perhaps the fact that he had been a seminarian had something to do with this. Perhaps the fact that they lived in the South during the early years of their marriage helped their tolerance level with each other's religion. Anita says she found the Catholic church of the South warm and welcoming, a fact that helped to create an inclusive wedding ceremony. Vows and blessings were exchanged in a spirit of mutual respect and celebration. This is not to say that the ensuing years of marriage have been easy. Walt and Anita have since moved north. As their family has grown they have experienced something of a struggle to pass on the Christian tradition to their children. Part of this struggle is that there are two conduits for this passage. And because the two traditions are very similar, they are faced with the hard questions of explaining the difference to their children. Is this all a historical accident? Maybe. Nevertheless, Anita and Walt have honored their promise to provide a Catholic education for their children. Still, there are special occasions when the whole family attends a service or a function at the Episcopal parish where Anita is a member. Their children, exposed to both local expressions of church, can see little, if any, difference. What they know of faith in Jesus comes from both parents, and if pressed, the children, both now pre-adolescents, would attest that the domestic church is the primary experience of church in their lives. It is through small communities of friends, their parents' friends and coworkers, that they have come to appreciate that Christians care for the world. If they understand that lay people have a ministry in the world, they have learned this from their parents, not from any concerted effort in the parishes. Anita and Walt, long involved in social justice issues, say that their churches have a somewhat narrow vision, one that sees authentic ministry as "doing church work." The issues related to the welfare of society and the commonweal, issues which first brought them together, are not central on the parish agenda. They remain central in the lives

of Walt and Anita, however. Yet, both agree that it is not constructive
or helpful to rail against the institutional churches, which are, in some
ways, bogged down by the weight of inherited institutional concerns.
They would rather stay within their traditional church affiliations,
locating the common spiritual ground upon which they can stand with
integrity. However, when the Spirit urges them toward new horizons of
freedom and responsibility, they cannot wait for the institutional church
to pass judgment on the rightness of the next step; or as they term it,
"We can't wait for the institutional church to catch up." When asked
about the formal and official dialogues between the churches now
underway for a number of years, they answer simply and humbly, "The
dialogues are a sign of hope, but a distant hope. Our common life is
a witness that there is more closeness than apartness between the
people of the churches."

Can we envision what women and men from different religious back-
grounds can bring to one another and to the wider church? In the practical order, I think of Protestants bringing their experience of pastoral
counseling: formulating the questions, spending time with people, suggesting areas for fruitful reflection and prayer. I think of Catholics
bringing their sense of sacrament, particularly the sacrament of marriage. And I think of the Catholic reservoir of mystical writing and contemplative prayer available for deepening the vision of God in
marriage.

While Catholics are at home with mystery and the transcendent, Protestants are comfortable with the practice of spontaneity in prayer,
caring fellowship with one another, and the familiarity of childlike trust
in God. There is a profound beauty in a family spirituality which
weaves all these elements together. When this happens in the family setting, the hope arises of joining different people together in the deep
reaches of the Spirit and of their offering each other fresh ways of
undertaking the inward journey. This is a sign of hope for unity within
the church and for Christians joining in common cause for the sake of
the world.

Again, Dr. Thomas reminds us that reflection on the meaning of marriage (theologizing) reveals a relevance for the wider community by
pointing to one of the major questions of our time: How do we live
together peacefully and creatively?[9] Within ecumenical marriages, this
question has a particular poignancy and a particular power.

Pope John Paul II seemed to understand the reciprocity between the domestic interfaith church and the local church. During a pastoral visit to the Netherlands, the pope spoke of the part local communities can play "in those important first years of married life, in which the spouses discover one another more fully and grow together in a life of faith which is capable of expressing not only an agreed minimal concord, but even an authentic appreciation of all that can be esteemed valid in the tradition and spiritual practices of the other."[10] The pope recognized interfaith marriages as potentially making a valid contribution to the work of reconciliation.

Domestic Church and Local Church

Families by their very nature provide a setting for spiritual growth and maturity. First, there is a relentlessness to family life. Like God, families don't go away. We may set forth, leaving family behind, forging new lives, but the truth is that the families continue to exist. This holy relentlessness forces us to face reality. For example, in Anne Tyler's novel, *Dinner at the Homesick Restaurant,* we meet the Tull family. Deserted by their father, raised by a stern and rather dreary mother, the three Tull children (now adults) who have never finished a meal in one another's presence finally do so the day of their mother's funeral—a day that also reunites them with their errant father. Amid their own anger and recriminations and defenses of one kind or another, the father, Beck Tull, confesses to his eldest and angriest son, Cody, that "when I left I didn't think I'd ever care to see you folks again. But later I started having these thoughts. 'What do you suppose Cody's doing now? What's Ezra up to, and Jenny? My family wasn't so much,' I thought, 'but it's all there really is, in the end.' "[11]

Second, in the day-to-day exchanges of domestic living all the sharp points of our egos are smoothed. To be a member of a family means to live cooperatively and collaboratively rather than independently. As family people we soon learn that every personal decision has a social consequence. From the food we eat to the friends we cherish to the way we choose to use our money, our personal preferences are honed into communal goals. The "I" chooses to move aside in favor of the "we." This may sound easier than it really is.

Several years ago my husband and I finally admitted that we needed a new set of everyday dinnerware. The wear and tear of twenty-plus years of family dinners had taken its toll. Off we went to a sale. Nothing on display really appealed to me, but rather than expressing how I really felt, I buried my distaste for the "institutional" china chosen by my husband, who I assumed wanted it because it was a bargain. We carried the dinnerware home, washed it, and put it all in its permanent place. The next morning, as I served the breakfast cereal in the new bowls and poured the coffee in the new cups, my whole being filled with tears. I hated the dinnerware. I explained to my bewildered husband that for me plates and bowls and cups are very important: I look at them every day. I need something beautiful, something I perceive as beautiful. Shocked as he was by my near breakdown over the bargain dinnerware, my husband suggested that we give the new, never-used (except for two cereal bowls and two cups) set to the Catholic Worker House in Washington, D.C. There the dishes now reside. When I related all of this to my spiritual director he pointed out to me how little collaboration was evident. I had approached the shopping expedition passively, not willing to get into the give and take of a decision. My husband had not sought to negotiate. We had both been locked into our own individualism. This dinnerware incident illustrated to me the strength of the ego that always seeks to control.

Third, families are our prime places of accountability. At home we learn how we affect others. Healthy families give feedback to family members. We come to see that our emanations may indeed be negative, but we would never know unless someone told us. When the husband of a dear friend of mine died she was thrust into sudden solitude. Even though she has a large family, the children were grown and busy about their own lives. She was alone, in an empty house. One day she identified the single most difficult aspect of her new widowhood. She said there was no one to reflect back to her her self, and there was no one to serve. Interestingly, this spiritual insight eventually influenced, at least partially, her decision to join a religious community of women.

In addition to these salvific conditions: relentlessness, ego paring, and accountability, the domestic church embodies and conveys, at least potentially, what might be termed countercultural values. Some of these values are:

being, over and against doing/producing;

sharing, over and against possessing;

creating, over and against consuming;
self-worth, over and against prestige or status;
mercy, forgiveness, and reconciliation, over and against revenge disguised as justice.

What the family is all about is shared life, and families make room for all kinds of expressions of life. Obviously, there is a tendency to slide comfortably into the right hand column. Possession, consumption, and status are not demons that are easily routed. But if we are faithful to our commitment to be present to one another, to be truthful, and to be open to influence (collaborative behavior), then we have a chance of living the left-hand column, and living it joyfully at that.

These same values are those that one hopes to see in the local church. Unfortunately, our congregations—gatherings of many domestic churches—too often resemble a well-run family business rather than a family that lives for others.

Within the family structure the experience of parenting represents a decisive movement toward adult responsibility. In absolute, visible ways another's life and well-being depend on us: on our wit and our willingness. Parenting moves us into a new way of knowing. How? For one thing, children force us to mature. Reverend Robert Hughes, gifted theologian and spiritual director, himself a father, is convinced that "no children get grownups for parents." Rather, he says, children turn their parents into the grownups they need them to be—or at least they try to. This is not to be confused with liberal permissiveness; it does not mean that children have or should have the ultimate authority in a family. What it means is that our children will try to turn us into the firm, fair, loving bearers of authority and tradition they need us to be. You might say that our children educate us. Furthermore, the education our children give us is not always pleasant. It can hurt. This education is one of the crosses that is specific to our vocation as parents. The very being of our children tests every chink in the armor of our psychosocial development as persons, and this testing is not unlike the "spiritual dark nights" of mystical literature. We are led to deal with the unfinished business of our childhood and adolescence through the gift of painful grace which our children mediate for us. The ground of our parenting experience is, I believe, trust. As we father and mother our children through all the stages of their lives we are called to levels of trusting we never dreamed we were capable of. Admitting that we are not meant to control our children, but rather to guide them and to be there for them, we are forced to let go of the illusion that we can control life. We find we must learn to trust the child, to trust ourselves, and most of all to trust God. When we have come to this place we realize we are standing on holy ground, standing in the truth.

There are some significant analogies here for our corporate life in the local church. Life in the domestic church, our families, suggests a checklist for the spiritual vitality of the parish (a list for both pastor and people). For example, are we allowing ourselves to be affected by each other so the divine wearing away of our egos can happen? Are we growing in trust of each other, respecting each other's competence and appropriate authority? Are we conscious of the subtle temptations to control, subdue, and manipulate others—always for their own good, of course? Is the parish a conveyor of those countercultural values listed earlier? Or does it resemble an efficient, smooth-running machine?

Perhaps the most significant question that can be asked of the local church is this: Does it appear conscious of its social mission, that is, outreach to the civic/cultural community? And does it act out this consciousness? These questions are also relevant for the church of the home.

Since the family is a true expression of church, one can expect that there is ministry within the households of faith. Prayer, listening and counseling, instruction, worship, works of mercy, the identification of members' gifts, the enablement and empowerment of one another, the caring for some segment of human need—all these ordinary Christian activities mark the home as truly a domestic church. Some concrete expressions of this ordinary family ministry include: parents praying for their children; one spouse encouraging the other to pursue new areas of study—and providing the practical household help necessary for the new undertaking; guidance and support of a child in his or her career choice, or lovingly challenging the choice; family Bible study; family action on a regular basis in the service of others (serving in a soup kitchen, befriending a refugee family, cleaning a retreat house, etc.). The possibilities for service and ministry are limitless, but it is not likely that families or parishes will see the possibilities until they are aware that mission is constitutive of their Christian lives. The pull toward individualism is stronger than we realize. But the surprising good news is that this sense of belonging to something larger than one's family tends to strengthen that primary community. "One of the Church's principal concerns in the area of marriage ought to be assisting couples to form relationships which are truly open to the concerns of justice and peace in the wider society."[12] This is a call to Christian families to minister not only within the boundaries of their own homes but to their neighborhoods and to the world around them. Still, it would be naive to think that Christian families will engage in social ministry without experiencing pulls in the other direction. The principalities and powers have not retired. Support for mission is one of the most telling arguments for the formation of small, face-to-face communities—basic Christian communities as they are often called.[13] (See chapter 6.)

Conclusion

What is the message of the contemporary Christian family to the local church? The message is one of affirmation of the personal content of marriage, of the knowledge of God that emerges from the deepest recesses of marital intimacy. The message is also that many deaths and resurrections are needed before one reaches these sacred spaces. This means countless reconciliations, endless choosing of the "we" over the "I," being stretched in trust to limits we never thought possible. The message is that creative ministry is needed for our particular moment in history, a moment marked by the trauma of divorce for many and by the new needs of one-parent families. How these families carry their burdens is often a powerful sign of God-with-us. The human and spiritual trauma of divorce often calls forth resources from men and women that they never guessed were buried deep within. Their suffering is frequently a source of grace and growth not only in their personal lives but in the life of the parish community as well.

The message is also that persons from different Christian traditions can live together in understanding and love and in service to the world. The domestic church in its many forms—forms as unique as the families who comprise the social unit we are calling the domestic church—stands as a prophetic sign that the larger church need not be impersonal, mechanical, or boring. The parish can tap into the energy and the reality of the family to release the wellsprings of new life. Equally important, the local church can put its many resources at the service of the family, enabling it to realize the nobility of its calling to be for others, especially those on the outskirts, those condemned to homelessness in one form or another.

Cody Tull, in *Dinner at the Homesick Restaurant*, falls in love with a most improbable woman, Ruth, a cook at the restaurant and a woman whose life is given to nourishing others. He comes to the restaurant to declare his love for her. Ruth is mystified. Cody could have "New York City girls, models, actresses . . . anyone." Ruth feeds him: vegetable soup, herbed salad, home-baked rolls. It is a feast for a man who rarely eats. In this kitchen-restaurant meeting, Cody has a most interesting insight.

> Couldn't you classify a person, he wondered, purely by examining his attitude toward food? Look at Cody's mother, a non-feeder, if ever there was one. Even back in childhood, when they depended on her for nourishment . . . mention you were hungry and she'd suddenly act rushed and harassed, fretful, out of breath, distracted. He remembered her coming home from work in the evening and tearing irritably around the kitchen. . . . She cooked in her hat, most of the time. She burned things you would not imagine it possible to burn and served others half-raw, adding jarring extras of her own design such as crushed pineapple in the mashed potatoes. . . . She ate little herself, often toyed with her food; and she implied some criticism of those who acted hungry or over-interested in what they were served. Neediness: she disapproved of neediness in people. Whenever there was a family argument, she most often chose to start it over dinner.[14]

Like their mother, the children were non-feeders, except for Ezra, the owner of the Homesick Restaurant. "There was something tender, almost loving, about his attitude toward people who were eating what he'd cooked them. Like Ruth, Cody thought."[15]

Families are asking their churches to consider: Are the churches feeders or non-feeders? And neediness? Does neediness trigger approval or disapproval? Questions to be lived with, honestly and humbly.

NOTES

1. M. Scott Peck and Gerald May are both psychiatrists whose work is situated

in the realm of the spirit. For example, see Gerald May, *Care of Mind, Care of Spirit* (San Francisco: Harper & Row, 1982).

2. Pope Paul John II, "Apostolic Letter to the Youth of the World," available from the USCC Department of Publishing and Promotion Services, 1312 Massachusetts Avenue, N.W., Washington, D.C. 20005.

3. Jack Dominian, "Person to Person," *London Tablet* (4 February 1984).

4. See J. Francis Stafford's intervention, "The Sacrament of Marriage: A Graced Covenant," given at the 1980 World Synod of Bishops. The text of the intervention is available from *Origins*, National Catholic News Documentary Service, Washington, D.C.

5. Robert Hughes, in a presentation on lay spirituality at the Glenmary Mission Center, Nashville, Tenn. (audiotape available from the Glenmary Center).

6. Jack Dominian, "The Use of Sex," *London Tablet* (11 February 1984).

7. Ibid.

8. David Thomas, *Christian Marriage: A Journey Together* (Baltimore: Michael Glazier, 1983), 74.

9. Ibid.

10. Pope John Paul II, "Address to Leaders of the Dutch Reformed Church," May 1985. The complete text is available from *Origins*.

11. Anne Tyler, *Dinner at the Homesick Restaurant* (New York: Penguin Books, 1983), 301.

12. J. Francis Stafford, "The Social Mission of the Family," intervention at the 1980 World Synod of Bishops. Complete text available from *Origins*.

13. Readers may want to contact Kathy and Jim McGuinness, directors of the National Parenting for Peace and Justice Network, 4144 Lindell Boulevard, Room 400, St. Louis, MO 63108.

14. Tyler, *Dinner at the Homesick Restaurant,* 160.

15. Ibid. p. 161.

FOR FURTHER READING

Leckey, Dolores. *The Ordinary Way.* New York: Crossroad Pub. Co., 1982.

McCarroll, Tolbert. *Guiding God's Children.* Ramsey, N.J.: Paulist Press, 1983.

Thomas, David. *Christian Marriage: A Journey Together.* Baltimore: Michael Glazier, 1983.

Vanier, Jean. *Man and Woman He Made Them.* Mahwah, N.J.: Paulist Press, 1984.

Young, James. *Divorcing, Believing, Belonging.* Mahwah, N.J.: Paulist Press, 1984.

3

Women: Changes and Challenges

> Social progress and changing eras are linked to increases in
> women's freedom, and social decadence is accompanied by
> a decrease in their freedom.
>
> Charles Fourier, French philosopher in
> Evelyn Sullerot, *Women, Society and Change*

Our Changing Era

THERE IS WIDESPREAD agreement that among the several social forces
unleashed during the past quarter century the change in women's roles
continues to gain momentum and is likely to alter the face of every
major institution in society. The change is profound and radical, reaching into the genesis of life and healing ancient ruptures and wound-
edness.

Clearly the changing roles of women include changing patterns in the
relationships between women and men in marriage and family life, in
the workplace, in legal structures, in education, in the church—in virtually every major societal institution.

Social roles and functions once thought to be determined and fixed
by sex are being exchanged and interchanged; both men and women are
developing skills and confidence in a variety of roles that were once the
domain of the other sex. This change or evolution is not simply that
women are leaving their homes to enter the job market. While recent
statistics show that more than half the workforce in 1984 was female
(80 percent of these women in low-level, low-paying jobs), significant
numbers of women, including Christian mothers, have previously

worked outside the home.[1] Women's presence in the marketplace is not the major change in our time. The change in women's concept of themselves is the greater change. More and more women see themselves as fully gifted, autonomous, and whole, able to define themselves in other ways than in relation to men.

I saw this firsthand about ten years ago. It was a cold, rainy autumn morning, the kind of morning that might logically confine a housewife to home. Contrary to logic, however, fourteen women, ranging in age from thirty to the midsixties, gathered in the Arlington County Adult Education Center to begin the first Seminar for Women under the auspices of the Arlington County Public Schools.

I had designed the seminar and convinced the school administration that it represented one response to community need. This first session was the trial balloon. I listened carefully to the bare outlines of the women's stories, which contained their reasons for braving both bad weather and a group of strangers.

One woman had been recently divorced. Twenty years ago she had worked as a bookkeeper. She thought she might take an updated bookkeeping course and then look for a job—but not just yet.

Another woman, a native of the Netherlands, the wife of a foreign service officer and the mother of a sixteen-year-old girl, said she felt herself slowly being painted into a corner of her kitchen. Coming to the seminar that morning was a first step out of her kitchen before the final brush strokes closed off her exits and entrances.

A sixtyish grandmother, recently widowed and the mother of four successful children confessed to never having finished high school. No one, including her dead husband, had ever known this—no one, until now. She had come for guidance and access to high school certification.

During the eight weeks of our coming together, I heard and watched the scraping away of some of the confusion and self-doubt which had accrued over the years. The seminar explored the fundamental existential questions: Who am I? Where am I going? How will I get there? What do I value and cherish? What do I fear? What are my immediate goals? What are my gifts? What have I learned from the experience of being at home and caring for others?

The women shared and evoked from each other valuable life experiences. They read authors, old and new, who were associated with the women's movement. They stretched their thinking and examined their assumptions. In addition they participated in aptitude tests and counseling sessions. It was a time of discovery, but the most important discovery was that they found they could learn more with each other than they ever could alone. Empowered by each other and their common enterprise, they discovered strength and courage, needed resources if the women were to make significant changes in their lives. What happened in that seminar was the creation of a learning community: adult persons drawing truth out of each other. Respect, care, encouragement, interest—these were the gifts these women brought to the learning community. I think there are some clues here for the churches' approach to education.

There were other fall and spring seminars, and the groups were fairly consistent in composition: middle-class, midlife women who had embraced the vocation of wife, mother, and homemaker fully and with great commitment. Now, in midpassage, many were alone: divorced, widowed, or childless, or in some cases psychologically and emotionally deserted by husband or children. Others were women who came to the seminars simply because they were beginning to feel the tug of autonomy, homemakers in the process of rearranging.

In class after class I saw how these women were able, in however small a way, to take some control of their lives. I also saw that the major institutions of society, including their churches, were not only unaware of their pain but offered nothing but the most superficial acknowledgment of their years of labor. The miracle was that the women themselves began to reflect on the value of their home-work and to help each other in the reflection process. They were going somewhere, together. I began to think of these women as pilgrims.

New Pilgrims

Pilgrimage, the metaphor I used in chapter 1 to describe the laity's growing interest in spirituality, is an interesting concept and especially apt for the situation of women today. The late anthropologist Victor Turner defined pilgrimage as essentially a movement *away from home, to a distant place, returning home again, with the pilgrim changed in some way during this process.* The dynamics of the pilgrimage engender change, particularly as a consequence of the profound experience of interdependence and egalitarianism. Turner calls the spirit which develops on pilgrimage *communitas,* and it is this spirit that returning pilgrims may insert into the static institutions of society; it is the spirit of belonging, of intimacy, and of unity of purpose.

The women I met in the Arlington seminars indeed forged bonds of interdependence. Their eight-week journey moved them away from home as it had been, toward unknown destinations, in the company of others who at first were strangers but who eventually became life-sharers. Their experience had the potential for bringing them to the threshold of a new and authentic maturity and for changing not only their homes but the churches where they worshiped and the neighborhoods where they lived. Freedom, like love, is diffusive of itself.[2]

These women represent a tiny fraction of the women throughout Western culture who are on pilgrimage. They are pressing the social structures for significant change, including fuller and more equitable sharing of the duties of home life by men, a recognition by society of the importance of homemaking as genuine work, and equal opportunity for meaningful work outside the home.

Edward Schillebeeckx tells us to look for the places and signs of liberation and freedom in the world, and there, he says, you will see the salvation of God at work.[3] Consider: Where are the places of liberation in our time? Certainly among people of color. Certainly among the poor, particularly in developing countries of the Third World. Certainly among women everywhere. And if Schillebeeckx is right, the living God is their liberator.

The churches, those pondering Gamaliel's question, Is this new development of God? (Acts 5:35–39), and trying to discern the truth, are those willing to grapple with the meaning of women's changing roles. If the social movement toward more equal and interdependent patterns of living and working is God's call to fuller human liberation, then the churches' prophetic and pastoral role is to further this movement or at the very least, not to impede it. Yet, if the church is to be the bearer of the gospel, then passive noninvolvement in the liberation of humankind is a bit difficult to understand. The views of Yves Congar, already mentioned in the Introduction, are particularly relevant here: the church today must be the asylum for humankind. In order to be an asylum, he says, it must be a *church for God*, preserving transcendent awareness (spirituality), and it must be a *church for the World*, participating in human liberation.[4] Both stances are essential, he insists. And I agree.

The prophetic responsibility of the churches requires cooperation with the grace of liberation evident in the changing social roles. In addition, the church also has a pastoral responsibility to men, women, and children to offer the stability of biblical conversion and support as well as the essential Christian values and truths as anchors in the sometimes distressing struggle for justice in an increasingly complex world. But to be both prophet and pastor there must be a willingness to live with the inevitable tensions that change engenders. There must be a willingness to face the hard, truthful, liberating questions. There must be the humility to experience and express repentance. All this is as true for corporate Christianity as it is for each of us as individuals.

Equality

We have certainly come a long way since Aquinas described females as misbegotten males. Contemporary theology, for the most part, is in agreement with the Vatican's publicly stated position regarding the equality of woman and man. "It is quite clear that woman was created in the image of God, just as man was . . . it is quite clear that both sexes were created together and that neither may prevail over the other in any kind of superiority relationship."[5]

Such church statements are in harmony with the work of sociologists who have studied the religious dimension of the evolution of sex roles toward greater equality. They cite Christianity as constituting a new charter of freedom for women, since it gave hope to all the oppressed, the humble, and the condemned. And they point to Jesus' actions as a foundation of this charter. Not only were women among his followers and close friends (Martha and Mary, for example), they were the first to proclaim the good news of Jesus' resurrection and were among the disciples who waited together in the upper room, in prayer and confusion, in those days between the ascension and Pentecost. But while initially the primitive church offered the women of the ancient world freedom from the confining structures of other cultures,[6] this was not to last. The history of the churches, by and large, is not a history of the equality of women. The Quakers are one striking exception, and convents, another. Within the Catholic tradition the freedom of women to define themselves as persons was perhaps most fully realized within religious communities of women where self-governance generally characterized religious orders and congregations.[7]

Within the last twenty-five years many official church voices have been raised in behalf of women's increased participation in the church. The documents of Vatican II, papal statements, the World Council of Churches—all speak persuasively to the principle of equality. Yet, despite this religious affirmation, there continues to be severe separation between the sexes. This can be seen most readily in sex-determined social roles. Studies in sociology and anthropology show that the separation has endured across time and cultures, almost always placing women in enforced enclosure of one kind or another and in subservient positions, while placing men in equally enforced dominant and competitive situations. A mutual pulling away from one another, the rupture of the original unity between woman and man, which some have speculated was the sin of Genesis, clearly continues, resulting in isolation and antagonism between the sexes.[8]

But what of the fact of Christ's redemptive life, death, and resurrection? Some speculate that these fundamental realities of our Christian life are gradually bridging the gulf between man and woman, enabling us to participate more fully and completely in each other's lives. There continues a burning hope, a hope for a more integrated way to be within families, within churches, and within society at large.

The Roman Catholic church has stated its unequivocal opposition to the ordination of women while still speaking out on behalf of equality.[9] In most of the Christian churches, however, ordination is viewed as a sign of the equality in creation of women and men, and of the eschatological nature of the church's mission. "There are no more distinctions between Jew and Greek, slave and free, male and female" (Gal. 3:28).

Some feminist analysis, however, would say that ordination is a diversion from dealing with the deeply unconscious but controlling fear of women that has engendered patriarchal structures in an attempt to deal with the fear. In a presentation on women in theology that I gave in 1980 to the Association of Theological Schools, I recounted a conversation with a Catholic priest who has had extensive experience in seminary spiritual and academic guidance. He has also been a consistent advocate of women's rights. Our conversation was about women studying for lay ministry. He said he was worried that if more and more women entered the seminary prospective male seminarians would be put off, thereby diminishing the already depleted ranks of young men preparing for the priesthood. As I thought over our conversation, and particularly his fears, I recalled the historical precedents for precisely the scenario he described. I recalled other professions or callings once the exclusive domain of men: nursing, elementary school teaching, librarian. When women entered these professions, men abandoned them. Would the same thing happen in ministry, and if so, why? Over the years I have posed this question to groups of laity, and especially to men. The general response has been that yes, most (not all) men are running. But there is less agreement about why. Nevertheless, it is a question as important as Freud's What do women want?

Dorothy Dinnerstein, a psychoanalyst currently working at Rutgers University, argues persuasively that men are profoundly afraid of women because of the necessary but difficult break with their mothers. Women must also break with their mothers, but it doesn't occasion the kind of rejection, denial, and repression that it does in males. Women can eventually be at one with their mothers and with other women because they are the same sex. In other words one recognizes self in other women without damage to one's autonomy and ego barriers. This is not so with males. The deep, deep ambivalence associated with breaking away from the primary nurturer and caregiver is carried all through life, making genuine, unself-conscious intimacy most difficult. Dinnerstein asserts that until and unless fathers are explicitly engaged in the care of the young and this male-female nurturance internalized by the child, men will not be able to dispel their fear of women, nor will we be able to alter the strong pull toward sex-determined roles.[10]

Young parents have gotten this message. More of them are opting for joint care of their infants and small children and arranging their lives to accommodate this value, often at great economic cost. It may be generations before the fear is uprooted, but the process is underway.

Women As Leaders

Meanwhile, women who have been ordained have been received in different ways. There are congregations which choose a woman minister and clearly value her gifted service to that particular community.

But I have heard too of women priests in the Episcopal church being not only ostracized but threatened. One of the most discouraging stories concerns a woman Lutheran pastor. Dressed in clerical collar and shirt she was paying a hospital visit to one of her parishioners and found herself alone in an elevator with a well-dressed middle-aged man. As she left the elevator he spat at her and verbally abused her in the most vicious way. Though she was physically and emotionally shaken by this episode, she was spiritually strengthened as she remembered the treatment of her Lord, the One she serves in the people.

Are the churches ready for women's leadership?

Is the world ready?

I hope so. The world, now at the edge, is in need of something else, something other than the fiercely analytical, righteous methods of governance that have led the planet to the brink of annihilation. The repressed or "lost" feminine principle is slowly appearing in the public realm, and not a moment too soon. The feminine principle, what is it?

I suppose Carl Jung is to be credited for bringing to our collective awareness the truth that each of us carries within us the sexual other. That is to say each man carries within himself a feminine principle, the anima, and that each woman carries within herself a masculine principle, the animus. According to Jung the masculine and feminine principles reside in the deepest parts of our psyches, bridging unconscious contents to the soul. Because they are hidden so deep within, the feminine and masculine components remain unknown. Unconsciously, however, we project the animus or anima content onto others. For the most part, man has projected the anima onto woman, and woman has projected the animus onto man. The result has been that woman has carried for man the living image of his own feminine soul, and man has carried for woman the living image of her own (masculine) spirit.[11]

Jung's is not only a personal analysis, but a corporate one. In a gender-separate society the conduct of public business, by men, has proceeded out of touch with the feminine principle. With the carriers of the anima at a distance, uninvolved and not easily influencing the policies of public institutions, the feminine (in both men and women), which Jung calls the soul, the spark of divine energy, is missing. Some call this the intuitive reality, the nonrational way of knowing, the artistic-mystic vision. And some assume that women are closer to this reality than are men, simply because the anima is familiar and not so alarming as it seems to be for men. Can it be that men are running from the lost part of themselves, that part symbolized by and crystallized around women?

Historian Barbara Tuchman, in an article in the *New York Times*, has written that the assumption of leadership roles by women is terribly important to the future of society.

Peace has not figured among the notable achievements of mankind. It is the most talked of and least practiced of all social endeavors. Men—and in this case I mean the male gender, not the species—are always saying they hate war and war is hell and so forth, and have continued to engage in it lustily, aggressively and ceaselessly since the beginning of recorded history.[12]

Mrs. Tuchman notes that, by and large, governments are made up of the male gender and if this situation remains unchanged, she is not optimistic about the governments of the world disarming. Tuchman's view is supported by the psychological expertise of Dr. Jean Baker Miller and the research of Carol Gilligan.

Jean Baker Miller suggests that the qualities which women *as a group* have learned in their domestic sphere (i.e., qualities of cooperative, noncompetitive behavior) need to be applied to the building of a just and compassionate society. Interestingly, Pope John Paul II holds a similar view. In an address to women he said, "I ask you women to transpose the exercise of these precious qualities from the private sphere to the public and social one."[13]

Carol Gilligan's research, presented in *In a Different Voice*, argues for women and men in partnership in all the institutions of society, *not* because of sexual sameness but precisely because of gender-related differences. Gilligan's work is a serious critique of developmental psychology, which has used male development as the norm. In previous studies the models for a healthy life cycle have been men. The mature men in these studies establish an important relationship between self and society, but appear distant in personal relationships.[14] The women in Gilligan's study describe themselves not so much in terms of universal principles or personal achievements as the converse, that is, in terms of relationships. The welfare of others matters a great deal to women, and concretely so. Gilligan, reporting about the women in her study, writes:

Identity is defined in a context of relationship and judged by a standard of responsibility and care. Similarly, morality is seen . . . as arising from the

experience of connection and conceived as a problem of inclusion rather than
one of balancing claims. . . . The world of self that the men describe at times
includes people and attachments but no particular person or relationship is
mentioned, nor is the activity of relationship portrayed in the context of self
description.[15]

A recent Gallup survey on faith development in the adult life cycle
picked up similar differences between men and women. For example,
significant life experiences, while important to both men and women,
are more likely to affect women's thinking about the meaning of life.
Women also differ from men in the kinds of support they turn to when
faced with a problem. Women are more likely than men to report turning to others for support or seeking help in prayer or the Bible. Men
are more likely than women to report working things through on their
own. It also appears from this survey that women are more likely than
men to reflect on their lives and to see religion as a very important
factor in their lives.[16]

It is precisely these qualities described in the Gilligan study and in
the Gallup survey—qualities of connection, caring, self-reflection,
interdependence, and recognition of vulnerability—that can bring new
light to secular and church arenas. It is a light needed by both church
and world. And, occasionally, church leadership is deeply affected by
the light.

As prophets we share in the prophetic mission of Christ to set people free in
truth and love by using every opportunity we have to proclaim that co-equality
and interdependence . . . of men and women in marriage and in the institutions
of society is the will of God. It is a fact that major tasks in society—
government, medicine, education, religion, child-rearing—can be accomplished best by men and women in co-equal partnership.[17]

With these words the U.S. Catholic bishops addressed the formal session of the 1980 synod on the family in which they spoke on behalf of
partnership. They are joined by the World Council of Churches in this
stance toward partnership between men and women.

A study undertaken by the World Council of Churches, "Toward
Fuller Community of Women and Men," implies that it is important
and valuable to strive toward understanding and reconciliation between
men and women. The WCC study was born of the awareness of broken-
ness in the community of women and men. It suggests to Christians a
serious issue, namely, how to work toward becoming a community of

equals, given the necessity of different roles within the community. The critical question is: How can we live in the realms of church and society in a mode of genuine interdependence and equality of influence? I suggest that one way is to become knowledgeable about the body of teaching on the subject of women's changing roles. For example, several documents of the Second Vatican Council contain the principle of equality. "Gaudium et Spes" refers to "new social relationships between men and women," and notes that since "women now engage in almost all spheres of activity . . . it is incumbent upon all to acknowledge and favor the proper and necessary participation of women in cultural life." It sees married life and love as "an intimate partnership." This teaching, now more than twenty years old, marks a distinctive development in the Catholic church.

Furthermore, since the council there have been a number of papal statements that speak of the equality of women and men. Some speak implicitly to the issue within the context of the dignity and freedom of all human persons, and some speak directly to the evolution of roles.[18] In addition, there are individual and combined bishops' statements that, taken together, form an impressive body of teaching. The 1980 International Synod illustrates this.

During that synod, two documents in particular were submitted that challenged both church and society. One, "The Changing Roles of Men and Women," was submitted by the entire U.S. delegation. It stated, "Co-equality, interdependence and complementarity of men and women in marriage and in the institutions of society are the will of God." (The term "complementarity" was criticized by feminists since in their view it reflected the idea that woman could not be complete without man, which they understand lends support to dominant-subordinate roles between men and women. They preferred the term "mutuality" in order to reflect an egalitarian position.)

The other intervention was submitted by Bishop Robert Lebel of Canada. He said that the church should be a leading place for the liberation of women, not simply a reflection of societal injustice; and that the church ought to denounce and correct all that brings about any form of discrimination or subjection. His final point was that true understanding of Marian dogma necessitates valuing the feminine in the church and he concluded by saying that women's equality in marriage, which was widely supported in the synod, can and ought to be transferred to other expressions of church. (Is this perhaps a case of "domestic church" influencing the wider church?) Finally, Bishop Lebel named sexism a sin.[19]

The prophetic voice from Canada was also heard at the 1983 synod, which focused on the theme of reconciliation. There Archbishop (now Cardinal) Vauchon of Quebec noted that civil societies, with the church's encouragement, have made progress in eliminating discrimination against women. Yet, he pointed out, "These appeals of the Church to the world for the advancement of the status of women as full members become simultaneously a reality within the Church itself; the Church needs to recognize our own cultural deformation and particularly the ravages of sexism and our own male appropriation of Church institutions and numerous aspects of Christian life."[20] The final report of the World Council of Churches in its study of the community of men and women speaks in a similar voice. Indeed, one could go on and on. The point is we need to become familiar with the growing body of public affirmation regarding the equality of women, the changing role of women, and the growth of human consciousness as regards the relationship between men and women and their alignment with the Divine.

Another way of behaviorally moving toward equality and interdependence is through dialogue. I was fortunate to participate in an ecumenical dialogue between men and women that focused on women in society and church. Several papers were presented, including one I authored that dealt with many of the themes in this chapter. Following the formal presentations were same-sex group discussions. I facilitated the men's group. The following quotations are in response to the question: How has your relationship with women (or men, as was discussed in the other group) deepened your relationship with God?

"Women have introduced me to God affectively. Men, cognitively. I've learned gentleness, the most important pastoral quality, from women. Most of all, from women I've learned to accept grace, and this from my wife."

"From my marriage I've learned about spontaneity and directness. That's like God, I think. God is not concerned with theories or words so much, but with our joy and our compassion."

"I've learned that God exercises gentleness and forbearance with us, and is often amused. I've also learned that God knows my cul-de-sacs, and will, when necessary, address my male drivenness and compulsive behavior. All this I've learned from women."

"Women are mysterious. This evokes the otherness of God."

There was agreement in my group that sexuality and power are closely related, for good and for ill, and that this is probably related to the awesome dependence of the infant on the mother. We agreed that some men never outgrow this dependence and continue to live it out, hostilely and otherwise, with the women in their lives: wives, co-workers, and parishioners.

One very gentle, intelligent, and painfully truthful man said that the evolution now underway is a serious threat to what women have been valued and needed for. He asked, "Who will show us how to be receptive to God?" And, "Will the 'new' replace that which we depend upon? What will happen to men? If women totally join us, and become like us, then we lose." The poignancy of these comments was not quite matched by the women's reactions, possibly because they did not have such a sense of impending loss.

In plenary session the women noted how difficult it is for women to express assertively and confidently what they feel they know. One woman spoke of the fear of abandonment if she really expressed what she felt to men. Most expressed the feeling of aliveness in the presence of a real relationship with a man. "I can hardly have a spiritual journey without the presence of the sexual other; my relationship to God and the sexual other are so intertwined as to be barely separable," one woman owned.

In response to the question, How are women to pass over to the experience of men who have a fear of women—and a fear of losing power? the group felt that women can speak of their own pain and thereby invite men to speak of theirs. However, they feared that often men would not acknowledge (or be conscious of) their pain and would reject such an advance from women.

These issues were never fully resolved in the group, understandably, but since it is a group that meets regularly although infrequently, I believe the agenda will continue to be addressed. All were affected by the beginning of a sensitive dialogue.

I think we need to face honestly the question of expectations surrounding women's leadership. For example, is there an expectation that women in leadership positions will act like men? That seems to be the assumption in many civil governments, and even in the churches. I am personally conscious of that danger as I move around the largely male world of a national church body. The danger lies in appropriating a language and a style that nuclear scientist Freeman Dyson calls the warrior style. The warriors, he says, are largely male, and they speak the language of efficiency and rationality, production and status. They are found in the military and scientific communities, he says, but elsewhere too. The warriors stand in contrast to the victims, who are, Dyson says, mostly women and children.[21] But I know how easily one can slip into warrior-ism. And I believe it will be tragic if we women lose our capacity to recognize our own neediness and vulnerability, and that of others. The truth, of course, is that everyone is vulnerable. Knowing it is the point. Knowing it is essential for spiritual growth. The spiritual pathway is basically moving from one level of vulnerability to another; and the paradox is that that is precisely wherein lies the strength. As a woman, my experience, biological as well as social, cultural, and psychological, has engraved that vulnerability in me. I think that men come to this knowledge more slowly. Sometimes it takes a midlife coronary to underscore the truth. On the other hand, we women need to see and understand that about men. We need to enter into a stance of empathy, a stance highly valued in the New Testament.

Women and the Future

What does the pain and struggle of women say to the churches? Many things. It speaks of the powerlessness of Jesus, an image surely worthy of the churches' meditation. It speaks of the centrality of persons, a theme at the heart of Jesus' life and mission. And it speaks of examining history with a truthful, undistorted eye, to see what really was, is, and can be. And it speaks of spiritual strength, a strength so deep and so true that it cannot be ignored.

Remember the Canaanite woman. Remember how she pursued Jesus, seeking a cure for her daughter? Many, many women can identify with the conversation between her and Jesus. First, he ignores her. He's resting, the Scriptures say. But she is insistent, infuriatingly so, and she makes her request again. This time Jesus doesn't ignore her—he refuses her. But it's not over yet. Jesus may have a goal, but she has one too, a deeply personal, concrete goal. It's not the grand, abstract goal that so often drives men onward, not anything like the destiny of Israel. Her goal is simply her daughter's well-being. What does she do? She moves in on Jesus, moves into his space so that he can't ignore her. She dares to interrupt his peace and quiet. And he says to her, "It's not fair to take the children's food and throw it to the house-dogs." Now, I suppose she could have left then, smarting with the insult. That's what I tend to do—leave when the rejection or the hostility is too much. She doesn't though. She says she's willing to take the scraps from the table. The woman is a study in tenacity. What drives her on? Love. Her love belongs to that wider and deeper love, which Dante sang "moves the sun and all the stars."[22] What we see in this story is that no one is exempt from the demands of that love, not even Jesus. He seems amazed at her faith and her transparent, tenacious love. He's caught in it, and it changes him. He changes his mind. The power goes out from him, and the woman's daughter is cured.

I think Jesus learned a lot about women that day, and being fully human (without compromising the fact of his divinity) and finally open to the encounter, he learned, I think, something about God, too. That's what love brings forth, always.[23]

The Canaanite woman's story is the story of all women. We owe it to all those who come after us to hang on with her tenacious love, a love that can move the world and the churches, as well as the stars.

NOTES

1. Cf. the work, which includes information about working mothers and the impact on family life, of Joan Aldous of the University of Notre Dame, Andrew Greeley of the National Opinion Research Center, and Rosabeth Kanter of Yale University.

2. St. Thomas Aquinas spoke of love as diffusive of itself.

3. Lecture delivered by Edward Schillebeeckx at the Trinity Institute (sponsored by Trinity Episcopal Church in New York City), January 1983.

4. Address by Yves Congar at the 1981 Congress of the Laity in Vienna, Austria.

5. Bishop Paul Cordes, on behalf of the Pontifical Council for the Laity in a presentation to the World Conference for the U.N. Decade for Women, Copenhagen, July 1980.

6. Cf. Evelyne Sullerot, *Women, Society and Change* (New York: McGraw-Hill, 1971) and Elizabeth Schüssler Fiorenza, *In Memory of Her* (New York: Crossroad Pub. Co., 1984).

7. This point is developed by Rosemary Radford Ruether in *Disputed Questions: On Being a Christian* (Nashville: Abingdon Press, 1982).

8. Cf. Michelangelo's Sistine Chapel figures. In one panel, Adam and Eve are reaching toward each other, the snake between them entwined around a tree. They are unable to touch each other or to bridge the gap.

9. The 1976 Declaration on the Question of the Admission of Women to the Ministerial Priesthood issued by the Sacred Congregation for the Doctrine of the Faith, Vatican City.

10. Dorothy Dinnerstein, *The Mermaid and the Minotaur* (New York: Harper & Row, 1976).

11. John Sanford, *The Invisible Partners* (Mahwah, N.J.: Paulist Press, 1980), 10.

12. *New York Times Magazine* (18 April 1982).

13. Pontifical Council for the Laity, Documentation for the Copenhagen Conference, U.N. Decade for Women, 1980.

14. Carol Gilligan, *In a Different Voice* (Cambridge, Mass.: Harvard Univ. Press, 1982), 155.

15. Ibid., 160.

16. *Faith Development in the Adult Life Cycle*, Module 1, The Gallup Organization, Princeton, N.J.

17. "The Changing Roles of Men and Women," available from *Origins*.

18. For example, "Familiaris Consortio," "Laborem Exercens," a 1979 address to the Italian Professional Association of Domestic Helpers, and Wednesday audiences of John Paul II as reported in *Osservatore Romano*, Fall 1979. Some of these texts are available from *Origins* (Fall 1980).

19. Robert Lebel, "The Sin of Sexism," available from *Origins*, National Catholic News Documentary Service, Washington, D.C.

20. Louis-Albert Vauchon, "Male and Female Reconciliation in the Church," available from *Origins*.

21. Freeman Dyson in a three-part series in the *New Yorker* (February 1985).

22. Dante Alighieri, *The Divine Comedy.*

23. The Council of Chalcedon declared Jesus to be "of one nature with the Father according to the divinity, and the same of one nature with us according to the humanity, in all things like us except in sin." This is quoted by Thomas N. Hart in *To Know and Follow Jesus* (Mahwah, N.J.: Paulist Press, 1984).

FOR FURTHER READING

Conn, Joann Wolski. "Women's Spirituality: Restriction and Reconstruction." *Cross Currents* (Fall 1980).

Gilligan, Carol. *In a Different Voice.* Cambridge, Mass.: Harvard Univ. Press, 1982.

Schüssler Fiorenza, Elizabeth. *In Memory of Her.* New York: Crossroad Pub. Co., 1984.

Ulanov, Ann. *The Feminine in Jungian Psychology and in Christian Theology.* Evanston, Ill.: Northwestern Univ. Press, 1971.

4

The World of Work: The Call to Co-Creation

> You must love your work, and not be always looking over the edge of it, wanting your play to begin. . . . You must not be ashamed of your work, and think it would be more honorable to you to be doing something else. . . . You must have pride in your work and in learning to do it well. . . .
>
> Caleb in George Eliot, *Middlemarch*

THE WORLD OF work, while one of the three principal arenas of lay life (the others being family and civic life), is often neglected from a pastoral perspective. Priests, ministers, and church leadership in general tend not to focus their teaching or preaching on what has been called "the marketplace." This is not to say that there is a total lack of theological principles regarding human work.[1] Rather it signifies, it seems, a failure on the part of the local pastor or parish Christian educator—those who regularly minister to the members of the worshiping assembly—to "pass over" into the experience of the men and women in their congregations who "go to work," day after day and year after year. An empathy gap? An understanding gap?

Co-Creating?

In the fall of 1983 the U.S. Catholic Bishops' Committee on the Laity attempted to discover the source of the seeming disconnection between religious faith and the world of work. Sixty laywomen and laymen were invited to consult with the seven bishops who comprised the Laity Committee. A few priests and theologians were also invited. The con-

sultation participants reflected a cross-section of Catholic laity who are
leaders in secular fields, although not necessarily leaders in ecclesial
settings. They included business leaders, politicians, men and women
from the field of medicine, the military, the arts, nonprofit organizations, labor, research science, education, sports, and journalism. Two
questions guided the planning of this consultative conference:

(1) What impact, if any, does Catholic faith have on your professional
life?

(2) What kind of ministry is needed now and in the future to help
busy lay people, committed to secular vocations, but also committed
to the church, to be consciously Christian in the world, and especially in the workplace?

The seven bishops who attended made it clear that they had come to
listen. They were conscious that the leadership of the church is not
involved in life in the same way that lay people are. And what did they
hear? Bishop James Hoffman of Toledo, Ohio, then chairman of the
Bishops' Committee on the Laity, succinctly described the conference.

> Our dialogue was candid, and the group was energized by its task. There
> was genuine love and appreciation for the Church and its role in giving par-
> ticipants a way of relating to life. As the consultation continued we felt a power
> and intensity: in the open forums that responded to the presentations, in the
> small group reflections, and during informal conversations. There was a sense
> that something was aborning and there was a desire to be part of it.

Many recommendations came forth from the work and faith people.
These recommendations were grouped into six areas. Bishop Hoffman
reported on these to the entire body of bishops.

> First, almost to a person, participants were grateful for the values and
> symbol system that they had received; they spoke warmly of the parish and/or
> school of their youth. However, they were not at all confident that we have pro-
> duced a renewed Church that provides the same symbol system that nourished
> them. Various pieces make sense, they said, but we haven't yet found the uni-
> fied whole that makes sense of real life.
> Second, there was a consensus that the parish is critical. Often the contem-
> porary parish does not meet their needs for spiritual nurturing, nor do homi-
> lies help them deal with key matters in their lives, nor does the parish fill their
> need for community. They see their vocation in the marketplace; they're look-
> ing for help in bringing their faith there. The Church, they said, has a respon-
> sibility to nurture their call through small Christian communities.

Third, as professionals, participants expressed a loneliness in their efforts to connect work and faith. The starting point is their daily experience—as attorney, as geneticist, as business leader, as actress—and that gives rise to the questions. We heard a plea for networking mechanisms, for mediating structures, including holding consultations on the subject of work and faith at the local level.

Fourth, participants asked for a fuller development of a theology of work, as well as a spirituality of work, rooted in the concrete experience of the laity.

Fifth, both men and women urgently called for the Church to listen to women affirming without reservation women's place in the work world. Participants urged recognition and support systems for working women and said that when the ministries are restructured, they should reflect the equality of women.

Finally, participants recommended the establishment of some permanent, active structure to make the wisdom of lay experts available to bishops and clergy, especially when they address public issues, and to alert the bishops to important new issues.[2]

Basically, these men and women said their Catholic Christian faith did impact their work life, but this was so because of the past: the strength of parish, the closeness of the Catholic immigrant groups, the formation they received in Catholic schools. Right now, they said, the church's ministry is missing them. They need and want the church to help facilitate small communities of faith where they can pray and talk about the meaning of their lives as Christian workers, and where they can also be supported in their family situations.

Sociologist and theologian John Coleman, S.J., who was one of the major presenters at the conference, picked up the people's themes. These reinforced his own observation that there is a growing tendency to privatize institutional religion, to put religion and economics, religion and politics, religion and everyday life in separate and distant compartments. Notably missing in this compartmentalist pattern, Coleman noted, is any sense of the transcendent. He is, however, opposed to what he calls "the quick fix": a program that makes you feel good for a while, or a program with no prophetic edge. Coleman believes this question—the decompartmentalization of religion and life—is so critical that we have to stay with it for the long haul. And the way he sees that we can is through Christian communities, men and women gathering regularly in a committed way and in small enough gatherings to be effective to "talk." And the talk will be a new kind of talk, he insists, because it will be asking the new questions, questions like: What is it in work, in family, in economics, in shops, in the laboratory that sings of meaning? What gives hope? What connects the various parts of one's life, and indeed of all life? And how do we come to see what "it" is? Is Shug right when she says "when 'it' happen to you, you can't miss it?"

This is the kind of questioning that can uncover the presence of God in all things, shaping a truly lay spirituality according to Coleman. "This kind of talk could transform our whole society, because if we did this a truly secular and a truly Christian spirituality would merge. People would be working with secular images and finding the 'it' there."[3] Not that people have not been working on their own to probe the meaning of everydayness, to seek to understand and be faithful to the call to co-creation. Furthermore, throughout the Christian era (at the least) there have been voices alerting us to the ways that the hidden dimensions of earthly labor draw us closer to God. These voices proclaim that one's work, wherever it is—at home, in the church, in society—is the site of vocation, of God's call in our life.

A Remembrance

I was fortunate to have heard some of these voices years ago when I first entered the world of work. I was nineteen years old. The portal to this new stage in life was the New York City Summer Playground Program. I was hired to be a counselor, which in practical terms meant a generalist, one willing to do anything and everything.

This may be hard to believe but as I walked to P.S. 136 on the first day of my three-summer career, bits and pieces of the church's social teachings, studied in the previous semester's theology class, danced in my head. In between encyclical phrases I talked to myself about the responsibility that pay carries with it and about how I would have to do my best for the youngsters who would constitute my group. There were even a few inner pastoral musings like, "God must want me to be a playground counselor because here I am and I don't even know the rules for volleyball." This followed by assurances to the unseen God that I would learn those rules and try to like volleyball. Most of all, I remember the excitement I felt during that early morning walk so many summers ago. I was on my way to work, to a real job! And scared though I was, my imaginative juices were running high.

P.S. 136 proved to be a microcosm of all my future work experiences and roles: teacher, homemaker, television producer, writer, and church executive. On the playground I met more than thirty energetic nine-year-olds. I met my own frustration, boredom, and fatigue. I also found there opportunities to stretch the limits of my inventiveness, my humor, and even my faith. The necessary tension of balancing work demands, social demands, family demands, and personal demands was first felt during those long, hot summers. Somehow all these legitimate demands had to be held together. I may have but awkwardly balanced them all, yet I knew I had to try. For in the midst of the tugs and the pulls there was a vague sense of vocation, of being called to do this particular work, not forever, but surely for those few months each summer.[4]

Several years later when I read George Herbert's poetry, it was like meeting a friend. His famous lines in "Elixir," "Who sweeps a room, as for Thy laws/Makes that and the action fine," have been words to live and work by. Herbert has helped me to see God's pleasure in the work of human hands, minds, and hearts, and to see the importance of the smallest details of everyday life.

Over the years, other writers have joined George Herbert as my tutors in the celebration of work: Simone Weil with her uncompromising attentiveness to whatever is at hand; Pierre Teilhard de Chardin with his mystic intuition. How often I have meditated on Teilhard's words: "God awaits us in every instant, in our action, in the work of the moment. There is a sense in which he is at the tip of my pen, my spade, my brush, my needle—of my heart and of my thoughts" (*The Divine Milieu*).

But some of my most influential tutors have been flesh and blood friends. As a young wife and mother searching for clues about how best to raise a family I was fortunate to meet a family who unknowingly provided a model for my family. I've written elsewhere about them, about a man and a woman who built a house in the woods of Minnesota:

They gave life to their children there, and taught them many things: psalms and poems and stories of great men and women. They taught their children respect for the intellectual life, for the spiritual life and for the life of manual labor. The man is dead now, and his grown children abide all over the earth. They are lawyers and writers, carpenters and artists, politicians, business persons and parents. They are caring citizens in a variety of communities.[5]

What did I see in that family? First, an atmosphere that valued creativity and the exploration of different kinds of work: the work of the home and the world's work. Sons joined their mother in bread baking, and the mother encouraged her artist son to find a corner of the house to serve as his studio. Politics, carpentry, literature, music— all were present in that household. What I learned from them was respect for diversity of work.

Now that my own children are grown, I see how certain learned beliefs influenced me. Among them is the conviction that the family is a primary place for coming to see that all are called by God to contribute to the world simply because of who we are (compassionate, ethical, spiritually alive persons) and what we do (how we use our talents). I believe a key to the family's vocation is in the willingness to support different members' particular vocations.

Clearly, much of my own appreciation of work as a means of knowing God has been fashioned in family settings, others' as well as my own. What I've learned within the four walls of home I've tried to apply to other work settings, and so I'm interested in the research of sociologists who see a significant relationship between the realm of intimacy (home) and the realm of tasks and work. For example, Rosabeth Kanter of Yale University is pursuing such questions as: What of their jobs do individuals bring home? What of their families do they bring to work? Questions like these echo the "new kind of talk" that John Coleman is urging.

Enabling Co-Creation

Unfortunately, I do not sense the local church frequently wrestling either with these questions or with the larger ones of life's meaning expressed through human work. Why not?

One reason may be that the energy of congregational leadership is primarily directed toward institutional maintenance. In practical terms this means that the preaching and the teaching are about Christian commitment in explicitly church settings: teaching Sunday school, singing in the choir, serving on the parish council or the vestry, managing church finances, and so on. After all, we are all subject to the pulls and tugs of self-interest both as individuals and as corporate persons. Another reason may be rooted in theological conflict. In other words, church leadership may not really believe the theological argument: that the world is good, shot through with grace; that God is available to us in our daily work; that our work can and should be a means of growing in the knowledge of God. The operative theology may hold that only designated sacred work really counts.

But at a much deeper level I wonder if a reluctance to place these questions at the center of the church agenda is not related to unfamiliarity with contemplative prayer. A contemplative mood allows us to see the intimacy between the individual acts of work and the ongoing creative work of God. That's why George Herbert's lyrics took the turn they did, and that's why Teilhard and Dorothy Sayers and Simone Weil and Pope John Paul II and a host of mystics of other generations could see the holy worldliness in ordinary human labor. If Evelyn Underhill is right in her contention that contemplation is everyone's inheritance from God, and I think she is, then the issue is how. How do we claim this inheritance and learn to see beyond the obvious?

One way is to be taught by another, one who is familiar and practiced in the winding and mysterious inner pathways. This is the most usual pattern in Christian growth: pilgrims helping pilgrims. In fact it is common in most religious traditions. Trustworthy guides, women and men who have themselves practiced the disciplines of attentiveness and concentration, willingly wait with others as they wait for God. In the past, one sought assistance from those who had given their lives to prayer: monks, elders, and desert dwellers.

But in our time, spiritual guides are just as likely to be our companions at work or in the neighborhood or in our church fellowship group as they are to be the official church leadership. Indeed, the priest or pastor may be as needy of guidance or direction as the members of the congregation. There are many surprises in store when we seek to understand who really is influencing the laity's spiritual life. One hears stories of financial counselors and real estate agents, supermarket checkers and dentists serving as caring listeners, encouragers, signs of God's joy and wisdom. In the course of simple, informal everyday encounters much spiritual guidance and solace are shared. How, then, can the priest or minister help? One way is to serve as a broker helping people find other Christians who are able to share the strength of their presence and the stores of their wisdom with other seekers. The pastor's overview position permits him or her to connect people with one another as few others can, but to do so requires more than superficial knowledge of the people of the congregation. She or he will need to know who is really knowledgeable and authentically reliable in the ways of the spirit and the habits of prayer.

But even this pastoral knowledge will not be enough. The pastor will need to reverence the giftedness of the laity and affirm them in their "second vocation," namely, their ministry of spiritual guidance—a service that may appear to benefit a few but which in reality benefits the larger community.[6]

The educational ministry of the parish can also affect the people's understanding of their life's work as vocation, and consequently as co-creation. Mark Gibbs has written about some practical steps that pastors and others in positions of ecclesial leadership can take to minister to their people-workers. Gibbs suggests that pastors keep abreast of continuing education opportunities in the area, such as a "Faith and Science Conference," and arrange for a scientist in the congregation to attend, subsidizing him/her if necessary. Often in the past it would be assumed that the pastor should be the person to attend, if anyone would. But as Gibbs points out, the parish person most engaged with science is the scientist, and it is he or she who needs to join with the best resources of the Christian faith to make the needed connections.[7]

Another suggestion of Gibbs is that the pastoral leadership learn the professions of the members of the congregation. This involves more than a master list of occupations; it means attempting empathetically to enter into the professional lives of the people. The effects of this learning are several. One could reasonably expect that the preaching would begin to reflect the real-life situations of the congregation; a pastoral sensitivity would likely develop, a sensitivity that would find its way into the pastoral counseling, the informal conversations, the shared life of pastor with people. A creative pastor might initiate or facilitate some professional reflection groups where people could do the "Coleman kind of talking." All is possible, but not without the willingness of the pastoral leadership to enter into this major arena of lay life.

Alienating Work: A Christian Response

Dorothy Soelle believes that it is a healthy sign that today people are refusing to do some kinds of work because they do not believe that just any work is good.[8] I agree. I know, for example, of television actors who have refused parts in a series because the roles denigrated the human person. I know of government workers who are seriously thinking about forgoing pensions and other benefits because of a growing crisis of conscience over the current United States military policy. And there are young couples who have deliberately chosen not to pursue the fast track to success but instead have chosen an alternative route, perhaps a lower rung on the economic ladder, in order to pursue creative work and to share in child care. Still others are choosing some form of volunteer ministry—for one year or two—spurred on by the search for meaning.

These men and women stand as prophetic signs in the world of work. And while every individual action is a powerful influence on both society and church, it also seems important and necessary that the whole body addresses the issue of alienation in work. This sounds like an issue for pastoral theologians, an opportunity to join Soelle in her expressed concerns. "If we are serious about acting as co-creators with God to fashion a more just world, then we must eliminate the evil of alienated labor."[9]

I have heard of some companies that are actively addressing the question of alienation. The lack of choice has been identified as a principal alienation factor. And so these companies, assembly lines at that (so I'm told), have given their employees authority to halt a production line or take a break. The first few days found the workers blowing the whistle constantly. The production line was definitely slowed down. But within a reasonable period of time, employees began to exercise personal integrity and responsibility, and production actually increased.

Soelle also points out that many work situations are isolated. "Another thing lacking is a neighbor."[10] By this she doesn't mean that people are so much physically isolated from each other as that they are emotionally and psychologically at a distance; and this condition appears to be enforced in the interest of efficiency. Christians who realize that the very meaning of life as mediated by Jesus Christ is that we are meant to live and love together rather than alone need to apply this principle to the work situation. Christian laity need to be helped by their churches to find ways to enhance cooperative living in the workplace.

Dr. Richard Fratianne, director of the burn center at Cleveland Metropolitan General Hospital, claims he has learned volumes about collaboration, about living in the body of Christ, since his appointment to that position.

> Because of improved medical care capability, we had many survivors. One thing became more and more evident: Patients left our unit devoid of interior life, their spirits dulled and, in a sense, condemned to a life of shame, with little hope. They were in many ways like the lepers in Scripture, the outcasts of society. . . . At that time in my life I considered myself a good Catholic . . . but [during the course of Cursillo weekend] what a revelation to learn that a personal and loving relationship with God was possible! It required learning to live a life of prayer. I don't mean prayer as asking God what He could do for me but prayer as a two-way conversation asking Him what it was that I could do for Him and in return receiving His grace to let me live it. . . . It became apparent that the only way that I could help my patients feel lovable was to love them as Jesus loved them. At first this seemed impossible but I slowly began to understand that if the Church is the Mystical Body of Christ, then Christians who band together for a common purpose can bring His Mystical Body to life. I began to experience and understand Christian community.
>
> But, how to translate this awareness into action? The medical needs of burn victims are so complex that it requires a highly integrated team of health care professionals to respond to the multifaceted needs of these patients. This group of very dedicated professionals includes physicians and nurses, physical and occupational therapists, adult and child social workers, nutritionists, hospital volunteers and the child life and education staff and our psychologist. . . . As the leader of the team, it was my job to take those things which we all shared in common, our individual expertise, our commitment and dedication to excellent care, and center that around an axis of Christian attitudes. . . . It was not a matter of preaching . . . but leading by example. . . . Team members were called to accept each other and their patients as they are, to be willing to share their burdens, to forgive them for their human weaknesses and to affirm their goodness at every appropriate opportunity. . . . we became united into a team. . . . the atmosphere in the unit changed from one characterized by pain, agony, fear, anger, guilt to one of peace, joy, faith, patience and hope. These changes occurred in all of us—staff, patients and families. We began to live 'compassion without pity; love without sentimentality.' We gained the ability to look past the surface ugliness and communicate with the inner person.[11]

Cursillo seems to have been the catalyst for Dr. Fratianne's initiative in trying to build a new kind of team within the burn unit. This new team is described by Dr. Fratianne as without dominants and subordinates while still recognizing different competencies. It is more like the community of equals that Jesus gathered around him.

It is this spirit of egalitarianism that bridges the isolation and alienation in work situations. This is not to say that no one ever engages in unsatisfying work. Drudgery is one of the inevitable aspects of most if not all work. The question is one of degree. No one should be expected to do alienated labor exclusively and forever.[12] As one scrutinizes the secular sphere, studying the signs of the times, one notices a growing concern for the personal well-being of workers. Seminars in stress management, sabbatical policies, continuing education opportunities—all these signify a value system that says the most important product we have is people. This is one of the signs of hope in the marketplace.

But what about those jobs that are continually tedious and not in themselves obviously life-giving? Mark Quinn in his article, "Five Guidelines for a Spirituality of Work,"[13] offers some concrete suggestions for tapping into the spiritual dimensions of monotonous or alienating jobs, for example, toll collecting on highways or bridges, or being in charge of the copy machine in an office. He says:

> In monotonous occupations the temptation is to disengage one's attention from the work at hand, and turn it instead to one's personal affairs. But the creative worker, rather than diverting ego from occupation, looks for ways to improve performance. He or she continually tries to increase speed and effectiveness, to upgrade the work environment with plants or music, to cultivate relationships with fellow workers.

Quinn believes that the more creative one can be at work, the more one can appreciate himself or herself there. And, he sagely notes, "appreciation is one form of love, the source, the dynamism of existence."

This approach centers on the worker, the person who lends dignity to every task at hand. There, too, is where Pope John Paul II continually turns his attention: to the person, the worker. In a talk delivered in Ciudad Guayana, Venezuela, the pope strongly defended the rights and dignity of workers. He said:

> The human person works because he (or she) resembles God. Among all the creatures in the world only the human person works consciously. . . . Actually, to work means to subdue or dominate the Earth, as we read in the Book of Genesis. All work, independent of its characteristics, has this purpose . . . work, all work even when one administers and directs the work of others, in a word, all of human activity: physical activity in industry, in the fields and

in services, intellectual work, the work of pure and applied research and so on has that character.[14]

In another place the pope speaks of work as the means of uncovering, developing, and increasing talents. "Work in a specific way forms the human person, and in a certain sense creates him or her. . . . It is the effort that is creative."[15] I have seen firsthand how this effort is creating a person's vocation in my own family. My daughter, Mary Kate, is an actress, and after she completed her fourth season of summer stock we had a chance to talk with each other about her future. I wanted to know what working in the theater means to her.

"Working is many things," she said. "It's being in a show, of course. But it's also the ordinary work that actors do every day between shows. It's practicing shows, exercising your body and your voice, auditioning, seeing people and making contacts, adjusting your resume. It's important to do a full day's work whether or not you're on stage," she insisted.

When I study Mary Kate and the life's work she's chosen, I see the difficult path her choices lead her: a minimal standard of living, few consumer goods, hard physical work, disappointments.

I also see the pure joy her work generates in her. When I asked her what she finds fulfilling in her work, she answered, "When I do the work well, I use every bit of myself to my fullest potential." And then she described a recent experience when she played in Chekhov's *The Seagull*. She said, "The moment came when I didn't think about what I was doing. I wasn't important—only the work was."

What Mary Kate describes is, I believe, an important element in any theology of work, namely a vision of self-expression and a sense of belonging to a larger reality. In other words, transcendence. In other words, co-creation.

A major question, however, is how to develop the awareness that our work is an expression of co-creation. In addition to Mark Quinn's suggestions above, I think there are several ordinary practices that can sharpen this contemplative awareness.

First is the practice of discipline. By this I mean the commitment of time, place, and attention to whatever task is at hand. This kind of discipline is needed for every kind of work, whether that be painting a room or painting a portrait. At the very minimum we all need to give time to the task. We have to come to the place of work. And we have to be focused and attentive in order for the work to get done.

Second is what I call the practice of common contemplation. By this I mean deliberately and fully turning our attention to our ordinary tasks of the moment: preparing tea, washing the windows, transcribing minutes. Simone Weil attributed her contemplative capacity to the daily recitation of the Our Father in Greek. The key was that whenever her attention wandered she would return to the beginning until she could recite the prayer from beginning to end with total attention. We don't need Greek to move in this direction. The contents of daily life can serve the same purpose.

Third is humility. St. Therese of Liseaux spoke of humility as living the truth. We can easily apply this to our work situations. How do we view the mistakes we make on the job? Are they experienced as a threat to our being? Or as a means to our growth and change? We know that great artists learn from their mistakes. I think great people and great workers do too.

Fourth is the respect for time, that is, realizing that time is the gift that tracks the flow of life. When we use time well, it enhances the beauty of our lives. To begin to get an idea of how we use time, we need to look at blocks of it: how we use time each week, each day, each hour. As we understand our use of time we are able to enjoy our work and do it well.

One of Mary Kate's acting coaches is fond of reminding her students that "acting means to recognize the life in yourself and the life all around you. And when you're on stage, to allow the life to resonate through you and show what it is to be a human being."[16] This teacher's statement is basically one of unity. It sounds very like the cry of Jesus that he had come to bring life, and abundant life at that.

If the value of our human work is lightly dealt with by the churches, so is the experience of sabbath. Sunday religious obligation and community laws against Sunday trade are of concern, but not the inner and outer experience of sabbath. This is sad. For not only do we need to appreciate and celebrate the work of our hands and minds, but we need to rest, truly rest, as well. I'm not referring here to the drivenness that characterizes so much of what we call recreation, but rather the practice of solitude, silence, nonachievement, play. The sabbath rhythm is a close kin to prayer.

For a long time I've thought that our pastors, priests, and ministers might be in a unique position to model for the people a balanced rhythm of sabbath and ministry, sabbath and work. But it may be that pastors, like the rest of us, need to learn to let go of continual activism.

Toward Mission

Lay voices talk about their lives. They talk about questions of meaning. What ultimate purpose does my work have? They ask: How do I come to appropriate the insight of John Paul, or theologians like Dorothy Soelle, or the metaphysical poets? How do I, a beautician or a musician or an accountant, come to understand that I am part of God's plan for the world?

A reasonable expectation, of course, is that the local church will be part of the search. Perhaps what is needed now is for the local church to adopt an intense listening stance, so that the vital questions about work can at least be heard. And then, perhaps, through humble prayer, an appropriate ministry can take shape.

NOTES

1. Cf. early papal encyclicals (e.g., "Rerum Novarum" and "Quadregessimo Anno"); Pope John Paul II's "Laborem Exercens"; the body of teaching on *work* from the Reformation leaders, particularly Charles and John Wesley and John Calvin.

2. Most Rev. James Hoffman, "The Bishop's Page," *Gifts, A Journal for the Laity* (Winter 1984). *Gifts* is produced by National Conference of Catholic Bishops' Committee on Laity, 1312 Massachusetts Avenue, N.W., Washington, D.C. 20005.

3. John Coleman, S.J., "Hopeful Realism," *Gifts* (Winter 1984).

4. The story of P.S. 136 first appeared in *New Catholic World* (June 1984). The issue was devoted to the laity.

5. Dolores Leckey, "Sacred Shelters," in *Living with Apocalypse*, ed. Tilden Edwards (San Francisco: Harper & Row, 1984).

6. Dolores Leckey, *New Catholic World* (June 1984).

7. Mark Gibbs, *Christians with Secular Power* (Philadelphia: Fortress Press, 1981).

8. Dorothy Soelle, *To Work and to Love* (Philadelphia: Fortress Press, 1983), 66.

9. Ibid., 60.

10. Ibid.

11. Richard Fratianne, untitled article, in *New Catholic World* (June 1984).

12. Soelle, *To Work and to Love*.

13. Mark Quinn, "Five Guidelines for a Spirituality of Work," in *Praying: Spirituality for Everyday Living,* no. 8. *Praying* is a supplement of the *National Catholic Reporter,* Kansas City, Mo.

14. Pope John Paul II, "Work and the Worker," an address given in Venezuela. Complete text is available from *Origins*.

15. Pope John Paul II, "Apostolic Letter to the Youth of the World," available from the USCC Office of Publishing and Promotion Services, Washington, D.C.

16. The story of Mary Kate and work first appeared as an article in *Faith Today* (October 1985) NC News, a religious education supplement for Catholic diocesan newspapers. It is reprinted here with permission.

FOR FURTHER READING

Bishops' Committee on the Laity. *Work and Faith in Society: A Handbook for Diocese and Parishes.* Washington, D.C.: United States Catholic Conference, Office of Publishing and Promotion Services, 1986.

Diehl, William. *Thank God It's Monday.* Laity Exchange Series. Philadelphia: Fortress Press, 1982.

Gibbs, Mark. *Christians with Secular Power.* Philadelphia: Fortress Press, 1981.

Gibbs, Mark. "Vocation, Work, and Work for Pay." In *Audenshaw Documents,* no. 32. London: The Audenshaw Foundation, 1984.

John Paul II. *On Human Work.* Washington, D.C.: United States Catholic Conference, Office of Publishing and Promotion Services, 1981.

Kanter, Rosabeth Moss. *Work and Family in the United States.* New York: Russell Sage Foundation, 1977.

5

Ministries and Mission: An Offering of Giftedness*

> The important thing is to recognize that our gift, no matter what the size, is indeed something given us, for which we can take no credit, but which we may humbly serve, and in serving, learn more wholeness, be offered newness.
>
> Madeleine L'Engle, *Walking on Water*

WHAT MADELEINE L'ENGLE expresses is something akin to my young actress-daughter's perception about her work as vocation, as a call so deep within her that she dare not say "No." But it also speaks to the insight or intuition that our talents are to be used for the good of the commonweal. The parable of the talents, a story which Jesus told in great detail, touches us so personally because we know it to be true. We have reservoirs of gifts that not only offer us fulfillment but can be "converted" or transformed into ministries and direct service—ways to carry forward the mission of Christ. This mission is to bring to men and women everywhere the good news that they are loved by God and are of inestimable value to the One who created and sustains them.

The stunning truth is that the liberality of our God, God's abundant grace, means that these gifts are poured forth upon all of us. How shall they be used? How shall ministry be animated?

Ministry? Appropriate for the Laity?

To Protestants the phrase, "priesthood of the laity," was and is as familiar as Wednesday night prayer meetings or the ancient hymnals. The theological grounding for talking about the ministry of the laity has long been in place. The challenge has been how to translate the theology into action, into everyday lay life.

One contemporary Protestant laity writer, David Specht, urges us to "live our lives as ministry." He sees God's people "ministering in their daily rounds of work and recreation, avocation and relationships," and he challenges the people to be not just thinking about ministry, but actually engaged in doing it.[1]

The Catholic theologian John Coleman, S.J., emphasizes much the same point. "Ministry is doing something. It is not primarily a status or lifestyle. . . . Christian ministry is an action . . . and [ministries] are a concrete service to the community in the power and name of the Gospel."[2] Coleman reminds readers about some fundamental Christian realities: (1) that ministry is a grace and gift of God's Spirit to the church and the world, reiterating the church's primary mission, namely the pastoral care of the world, and (2) that in order for the mission to be accomplished a great variety of ministries will exist and grow in the context of community. The emphasis here, is on variety. This is, of course, the theology of 1 Corinthians 12 where ministries are rooted in gifts and flourish in wonderful diversity. Madeleine L'Engle expresses the image of diversity and unity this way:

> We all feed the lake. That is what is important. It is a corporate act. . . .
> In the theater I was never more than an understudy or bit player . . . but I knew
> the truth of Stanislavsky's words: 'There are no small roles. There are only
> small players.'[3]

Ministry is a new word for Catholics; a familiar one for Protestants. For all of us lay people it is a word that challenges the very heart of our Christian lives.

One morning in the mid-sixties, as I served cereal to four very young and very lively children, I opened the *Washington Post* to a surprising story. The word from Rome was that the laity shared in the priesthood of Christ. I looked around the disheveled breakfast table at four momentarily serene, small faces and let the wonder of it sink in. "The laity are sharers in the priestly, prophetic and kingly functions of Christ. They carry out their own part in the mission of the whole Christian people with respect to the Church in the world."[4] So spoke the fathers of the Second Vatican Council.

There was more in the *Post* story: talk of charisms and rights of believers, and a council calling for the people to use their talents for the welfare of society and the upbuilding of the church. I glanced at my bookcase of pre-Vatican II theology, one Yves Congar volume wedged among the scholastics, and lingered longer than usual over the morning paper, indifferent to the mayhem mounting under my feet. The news was something to ponder. Indeed, across the Catholic world men and women began to ponder, to question, to draw up plans of action for coming to grips with our newly clarified Christian lay identity.

One heard little, if any, talk of "ministry" in relationship to the laity in the early council days, at least among Catholics. There was, however, considerable talk of the laity's spirituality, that is, the witness of life at home, in neighborhoods, in the workplace, in public institutions, in the arts, and so on. There was talk, too, of "mission," a term often used in documents of Vatican II. It was a concept that felt right for laymen and laywomen who had been involved in Catholic action and the apostolate. In the United States the civil rights movement provided a natural locus for the energies of socially idealistic young Catholic families and equally idealistic parish priests, now savoring the streams of good news flowing from the council.

While the pragmatic foundations of shared responsibility for the mission of the church were squarely set in the social justice arena, the church was also presenting itself differently on other fronts. The look of the Sunday morning sanctuary changed, for example. Laymen and laywomen joined the priest in reading the Scriptures and distributing Communion. And now they were called ministers, lay ministers. Soon the laity were ministering with youth groups, social concerns committees, family life offices, on college campuses, in jails and hospitals— everywhere that priests and religious had been the exclusive bearers of the gospel message.

This was the new reality in 1977 when I arrived at the National Conference of Catholic Bishops as the first director of the U.S. Bishops' Committee on the Laity. Lay ministry was a priority on the bishops' agenda. There were few specifics attached to the concept, but there was the conviction that lay ministry was to be encouraged, that it had considerable energy behind it, and that it was of the Spirit. The committee believed lay ministry deserved study and reflection.

What did I learn? First, many Catholic dioceses were committing themselves to a variety of lay ministry formation programs. The impetus seemed to be a combination of several forces: one, the declining numbers of priests and religious now available; another, the people's need for a variety of ministries; and yet another, the theological imperative for all to share actively in ministry. Such programs continue to increase yearly.

I also discovered that sizable numbers of young and midcareer adults were and are in colleges and universities, in seminaries and divinity schools, and in institutes of pastoral ministry, preparing for professional lay ministry. Their goal is to work full-time for the church in a pastoral capacity. They are investing their time, energy, and money toward realizing their vocational goals. And most striking, in their quest for meaning they are willing to forgo the security that other professions can offer. Their numbers continue to grow: witness the many parish, diocesan, and institutional ministries that are now staffed by lay persons. Alongside this population are volunteer lay missioners of all ages, serving in the foreign and domestic missions for a specified period of time, typically in association with a religious order. All reports indicate that a returning lay missioner's experience of church is radically changed and he or she brings to the parish a new set of expectations regarding ministry and regarding the mission of the church.

I also learned that the meaning of lay ministry always engenders spirited discussion. Is lay ministry only identifiable church ministry? Can the laity's ordinary life and work rightly be called ministry? Should it be? Where did that word come from anyway? Furthermore, in conversations with Protestants who were not facing the acute personnel problem that Catholics were and are, and who were not so bound up in issues of women's ministry and the place of authority in the church, lay ministry did not seem caught in the same complex web as it did in Catholicism.

In 1980 the Bishops' Committee on the Laity offered its reflections on the development of the lay role in the church since Vatican II. Its pastoral statement on the subject, *Called and Gifted*,[5] approved by the entire body of bishops, identified the laity as called by God to life in the church that is characterized by adulthood, holiness, ministry, and community. It is interesting and significant to see how the ministerial section is organized. It begins with the statement that baptism and confirmation empower all believers to share in some form of ministry. The bishops go on to speak first about the laity's call to ministry in the world.

> The whole church faces unprecedented situations in the contemporary world, and lay people are at the cutting edge of these new challenges. It is they who engage directly in the tasks of relating Christian values and practices to complex questions such as those of business ethics, political choice, economic security, quality of life, cultural development, and family planning. . . . In those areas of life in which they are uniquely present and with which they have special competency because of their particular talents, education and experience, they are an extension of the church's redeeming presence in the world.

It is not until after the laity's normative secular ministry is affirmed that the bishops speak about the laity's call to ecclesial or church ministry. Here the ministry of catechist, parish and diocesan councilor, eucharistic minister, spiritual director, as well as full-time professional minister, is acknowledged with gratitude. What *Called and Gifted* offers is an inclusive view of lay ministry. The laity's church service is ministry, but so is everyday life and work, and preeminently so.

Purists of the left and the right have been troubled by this twofold description of the laity's ministry. Why? I think there are three reasons, at least. First, there is a question of language; second, a question of image; and third, a question of ecclesiology.

Language

The truth is that language is always changing; semantic shifts are a fact of linguistic life. Not only are words added and lost in any given lexicon, but the meanings of words over time are narrowed or broadened. For example, "companion" once referred to a person with whom one shared bread; today it means a person who accompanies another. The word "ministry" seems to be in the middle of a semantic expansion pushed by the reality it is trying to convey.

Images

Clearly, images of ministry have been fixed to a certain extent within the Catholic psyche by pre-Vatican II images of priest-minister and

vowed religious. These were images of ministers markedly different
from the rest of the church body. They dressed differently; they lived
in different kinds of homes; their lives were peaceful and ordered (or
so we thought). With this singular pattern in mind lay ministers are
sometimes thought of as equally churchbound and different from the
rest of the parish community. Some think of lay ministers as busy at
"churchy" tasks, divorced from the claims of civic and social life—an
image disliked by many laity. This image tends to change, however, as
parish or diocesan ministry becomes a shared enterprise and lay
ministers are experienced as they are, not as they are imagined. The
lay minister who is responsible for the parish prayer group or the parish
council or eucharistic ministry or religious education or pastoral counseling often holds down a full- or part-time job, cares for a family,
attends the symphony, frequents the library, and works in political cam-
paigns. In short, he or she leads a typically complex lay life. As in so
many other areas, we have to be willing here to discard old and worn
images, and let the edges of the new appear.

Ecclesiology

The question of living out Vatican II's vision of the church is not isolated from the issues of language and image, but, in fact, all three affect
each other. If we believe with the council that the church exists to carry
on the mission of Christ and if we believe with the council that laity
are joined with priests and vowed religious as enactors of that mission,[6]
then what we have is a church of ministers: some of them clergy, some
of them religious, and most of them laywomen and laymen. Such an
ecclesiology allows for the richness of varied ministerial roles which
will create fresh images. It is at this point that a reflective parish needs
to examine its corporate conscience to uncover whether or not the
parish is guided by the fullness of the council's ecclesiology.

A Conscious Community of Ministers

What might it mean for a particular parish to be a conscious community of ministers? I have identified four characteristics or behaviors that
seem to me essential and that I believe are applicable to parishes and
congregations in other Christian traditions.

First is the quality of Sunday worship. All of the roles in the Sunday liturgy should be undertaken with care and adequate preparation. Since they are transmitting the symbols of the Christian faith, the priest and other liturgical ministers have a serious responsibility to preside as well as they possibly can. This includes preaching built on knowledge of the people in the congregation, their needs, hopes, desires, and fears, as well as on knowledge of the Scriptures, theology, history, and so on. It is equally important that the preacher be familiar with the world of the Spirit, that world which he invites others to explore. Evelyn Underhill once said to pastors, "Your people will know in a minute if God is real to you." I think that is still true.

Second is intentional fostering of lay spirituality. While this certainly means a commitment on the part of parish leadership to pray for the people ceaselessly, it also means making available to the people quality spiritual direction and counsel. The people will know if the pastor and other priests are equipped to take this task seriously. Still, there are limits to what even the most generous priest can do, and so, as discussed in the previous chapter, good pastors will try to identify others who are so trained and endowed and will encourage them to use their gifts on behalf of others. A parish that cares about developing lay spirituality will also foster faith-sharing groups to help people live out their family, work, and civic responsibilities from a spiritual center. Opening ecclesial ministries to more and more people is yet another practical means for developing lay spirituality. As Baptists have consistently shown, direct service to others remains one of the tested and true ways for growth in the spirit. Of course there are dangers in opening wide the doors to ecclesial ministry. Like anything else, it can be used as an escape from primary relationships and duties, but presumably wise parish leadership would be alert to that possibility.

Third is ongoing adult theological education. There really cannot be a ministering community without such opportunities. Lay people need resources for developing their theological expertise to complement other areas of competence. This may mean, as Mark Gibbs suggested, that the parish underwrite the cost for businesspersons, scientists, politicians, and so forth to attend workshops and conferences. It might mean theology courses regularly offered at times, places, and costs convenient for the laity. It will almost certainly mean hiring a staff person to attend imaginatively to this critical area of parish life.

Fourth is a focus on the parish's mission to the world. Through preaching, education, and spiritual formation a spirit of outward mission can be nurtured and helped to find concrete expression. Organizationally this might look like a network of mission groups compassionately engaged with whatever segment of human need God directs them toward. Grounded in prayer and study, the people can be motivated to act together as a gathered church, or individually as members "on mission" (for example, tutoring or visiting the homebound). The role of pastoral leadership is to keep before the groups and the people as a whole the gospel vision of our need to ally ourselves with the poor and the powerless. Without this kind of leadership, small communities could become narcissistic enclaves, meeting to shield one another from the challenge of change.

The Gift of Ministry

It is evident, I think, that community is an essential ingredient for vital mission and gifted ministry—and that is the subject of the next chapter. But the subject for our reflection now is the reclaiming of mission and ministry as central to Christian life—for all Christians. Surely it is ultimately God who calls us to participation in and responsibility for that which Jesus called the kingdom of God. Surely it is ultimately the Spirit who stirs our giftedness, suggesting a mission and a ministry. Sometimes the church, if it is a congregation converted to mission, is the means of our hearing and the enabler of our response. Sometimes—oftentimes—a layperson is the needed bridge from private Christianity to mission. My friend, Jean Sweeney, now a pastoral counselor in a Catholic parish, formerly director of the Northern Virginia Literacy Council, is serving as my bridge.

My work with the National Conference of Catholic Bishops is steeped in church meetings, church readings, church people. An extensive travel schedule, a home to care for, and a husband to share life with are enough responsibility for anyone, I've told myself. Furthermore, the children may be adult, but they're still studying, still in formation. They need whatever time and energy are mine to give. Not only that, I mentally trot out my past record, filled with ministry and mission. There are our civil rights and fair housing work, hospitality to foreign students, our sponsorship of a parolee. And I say to myself that these were the ministries of my younger days; now I do the work of the church, work for which I am paid. Isn't that a form of mission? Some would answer "yes" to this question, and in some ways they are right, for my work in the church feels, grows, and develops the way vocations do—the way Mary Kate "recognizes the life in herself and the life all around." But I know there is a missing piece: a direct, personal engagement in some segment of human need.

If ministries are, indeed, related to our giftedness as has been argued in this chapter, an important step in discernment is the identification of one's gift or gifts. In my own case, I have always recognized teaching as a gift, whether the setting be a high school English class, pastoral theology in graduate school, or any variety of adult education. The teaching-learning relationship is full of energy for me and, as I have found, full of hope, no matter what the specific content may be. Enter Jean Sweeney!

Jean and I have met, off and on for many years, to pray, read Scripture, and talk about our Christian journeys. During the past year our meetings have been quite regular, and so my mission gap has occasionally been part of our conversation. One day, Jean gave me *Letters by a Modern Mystic,* the correspondence of Frank Laubach, a Methodist missionary to the Philippines. This little book was offered because I had been making inquiries about the Literacy Council. Jean was providing background. I learned that in 1930 Dr. Laubach went to Dansalan in the uplands of Mindanao in the Philippines to begin a remarkable service with the Moros, Islamic natives of the island. Dr. Laubach's wife and infant son were not with him, and so he faced a new and uncertain mission alone. Not totally alone: God, it became evident, was with Laubach in a most extraordinary way. In the milieu of solitude Laubach was led into the deepest mystical experience with God and the deepest friendship with the Moros.

It was not long before the Moros realized the nobility of spirit of this American who had come among them. And what did Laubach find? He found the Moros almost entirely an illiterate people. Yet, by 1937 one-half of the 90,000 who lived about the lake could read and write. Laubach devised a remarkably effective method of adult education, one still used in literacy programs all over the world, one used by my friend, Jean. Alone, Laubach helped his new Muslim friends develop industries, improve agriculture, and attend to health services. It is generally held by all who knew Dr. Laubach that this all came to be because he opened himself to the spirit of God as an effective channel for the outflow among needy people of God's transforming power.

During his early months on Mindanao, Dr. Laubach wrote a number of letters to family and friends. It is there that we see the soul of the mystic, the man engaged in inner work, the man drawn to ministry, the man experiencing oneness with the primitive Moros. In one of his letters he wrote:

> I do nothing that I can see excepting to pray for them, and to walk among them thinking of God. They know I am a Protestant. Yet two of the leading Moslem priests have gone around the province telling everybody that I would help the people to know God.[7]

Frank Laubach's attention to his inner work (the spiritual search), the minute-by-minute awareness of God, intensified his awareness of others. "People over all the world are withering because they are open toward God only rarely. Every waking minute is not too much."[8] His spiritual work not only pointed to his mission but connected him to the energy of God for the carrying out of the mission. His creativity flowed from the source of all creativity. His mission sense reached to the far corners of the world; and it grew out of a question which he believed to be most important: Is God your friend? Laubach believed that as with all friendships one has to spend time with God in order to be able to communicate comfortably.

I have read and reread Laubach's letters And more and more I am drawn to move in the mission stream that he generated. The adult literacy motto is "Each one teach one," clearly a personal, hands-on ministry. Christian friends say, "Finish that book you're working on [*Laity Stirring the Church*] so all the blocks will be cleared away." Jean, knowing my recent efforts at learning Spanish, suggests I take the kind of literacy training that will qualify me to work with Hispanic adults, helping them one at a time to speak and to read English. There will be a degree of mutuality in this ministry, she points out, an indicator of integrity and community.

The time has come to heed the wisdom of my lay friends. When this manuscript is finished—hopefully soon—I will discover first hand the method Frank Laubach learned in the depths of his heart:

When you are teaching the Moros to read, your art is to say as little as you can and leave them to say as much as they will. That is why I leave you to do and say as much as you can, while I say little. You learn by doing, even when you make mistakes and correct them. . . . This is the best way to act: Talk a great deal to me. Let others talk a great deal to you, appreciating everything fine they say and neglecting their mistakes.[9]

A World in Need of Ministry

My new step, something I anticipate with genuine joy, has been illuminated and clarified for me, and encouraged by my lay companions along the way. Even though the adult literacy ministry occurs on a one-to-one basis, it is still part of a larger mission, and it has a deep influence on cities and towns and other communities wherever it exists. One way to gain some insight into the kind and extent of the local church's mission is to ask whether or not the community in which the church lives would be poorer should the church suddenly disappear. The issues are whether or not the church is caring for society and how well it does that.

Active corporate mission in these last years of the twentieth century, if not widespread, is happening, and it is focused on several major concerns. The escalating nuclear arms race is one. Here, the collective voice of the Catholic bishops[10] joins other, smaller activist groups who consistently have opposed in word and in deed the nuclear madness. The traditional peace churches (e.g., the Quakers and the Church of the Brethren), the Sojourners community, the Catholic Worker—all these keep the vision alive that a nuclear-free world is possible and that Christians have a part in making it so. The plight of Central America is another point of mission for many Christians. From Witnesses for Peace, who literally put their bodies on the line between Honduras and Nicaragua in a search for the truth, to missionaries (including lay missionaries), to the growing number of churches and Christian communities that are offering sanctuary for political prisoners from Central and South America, Christians are strengthening their bond with the least of their brethren. In major urban areas Christians have joined together to offer shelter for abused women and children and to try to deal with the root cause of this violence. And all across the land other Christians have joined with Catholics in opposing abortion and finding alternatives to that desperate act. Still, this is the tip of the iceberg.

Sometimes I wonder what would happen if all 19,000 Catholic parishes in the United States were to declare themselves on mission to the world. What would happen if these parishes and all the Protestant and Orthodox congregations intentionally and intelligently set about to befriend the polluted rivers and the threatened outer space? Or to befriend the growing numbers of refugees seeking sanctuary and a new life in the United States? What would happen if every white Christian community bonded with our black brothers and sisters in the cities and the farmlands and as far away as South Africa? Might it happen that the world would glow a little from the transfiguring light that bathed the holy mountain so many nights ago?

A more urgent question is how can it happen?

There may be a way.

NOTES

*Portions of this chapter appeared in my article, "The Ministry of the Laity: Language, Image and Reality," *Church* (January 1985), published by the National Pastoral Life Center, New York.

1. David Specht, "Editor's Note," *Centering* 2, 3 (Spring 1985); published by the Center for the Ministry of the Laity, Andover Newton Theological School, Newton Centre, Mass.

2. John Coleman, S.J., "A Theology of Ministry," *The Way* (January 1985).

3. Madeleine L'Engle, *Walking on Water* (New York: Bantam Books, 1982), 196.

4. "Lumen Gentium," art. 31, in *Documents of Vatican II*, no. 40.

5. *Called and Gifted: Reflections of the American Bishops Commemorating the Fifteenth Anniversary of the Issuance of the Decree on the Apostolate of the Laity*, 1980. Available from the United States Catholic Conference Office of Publishing and Promotion Services, Washington, D.C.

6. "Decree on Missions," in *Documents of Vatican II*.

7. Frank Laubach, *Letters by a Modern Mystic* (Syracuse, N.Y.: New Readers Press, 1979), 28.

8. Ibid., 24.

9. Ibid., 40.

10. *The Challenge of Peace: God's Promise and Our Response, A Pastoral Letter on War and Peace*, by the National Conference of Catholic Bishops. Available from the USCC Office of Publishing and Promotion Services.

FOR FURTHER READING

Church, a bimonthly publication of the National Pastoral Life Center, New York, N.Y.

Dunning, James B. *Ministries: Sharing God's Gifts.* Winona, Minn.: St. Mary's Press, 1980.

Kinast, Robert. *Caring for Society.* Chicago: Thomas More Press, 1985.

O'Meara, Thomas, O.P. *Theology of Ministry.* Mahwah, N.J.: Paulist Press, 1983.

Peck, George, and John S. Hoffman, eds. *The Laity in Ministry.* Valley Forge, Pa.: Judson Press, 1984.

Growing Together. This publication contains the proceedings of a 1980 national conference on shared ministry. Available from the Office of Publishing and Promotion Services, United States Catholic Conference, Washington, D.C., 1980.

Ministry Development Journal, A Publication of Education for Mission and Ministry, Episcopal Church Center, New York, N.Y.

6

Community: Gathered in Christ for the Sake of the World

> Friendship, like any relationship, requires work and attention, the ability to change and to reorder a relationship if necessary so that it is built on reality instead of illusion.
> Susan Wood, "The Family of Friends,"
> *Washington Post*, September 1985

At St. Trudo Abbey—Belgium

IN JUNE 1985 approximately seventy Catholic men and women (and two Protestants) gathered in a symposium held in the Abbey of St. Trudo, outside Bruges, in Belgium. The abbey, a living abbey—home to thirty canonesses—readily reminds one of the monastic stream that has passed on the rich tradition of Catholic spirituality from generation to generation since the time of Saint Benedict.

From five continents we came to St. Trudo's to study and to learn together what we as Christians must do, in these last years of the twentieth century, so that true communities of faith may grow and prosper and the church may shine as the light on the hillside.

For six days we lived in small, stable groups: African, Asian, European, North American, and South American. In these temporary face-to-face communities of different cultures and different experiences, we listened to the symposium faculty relate the history, the theological development, and the social analysis of Christianity. More important, perhaps, we listened to one another.

Sister Regina, a Filipino, related to us her work with basic Christian communities in the Philippines. These communities work with political

99

prisoners and their families, trying to bring hope and compassion to the most abandoned. One evening during the symposium we did not work in our groups. Relaxation time was declared. We went together to visit the beautiful medieval city of Bruges: the churches, the Beguinage,[1] the museums. It was good to enter into the historical reality of the city. In the hour before our dinner together in a designated hotel, people broke once again into small groups to enjoy an aperitif and some quiet conversation.

The next morning, in our work group, Sister Regina spoke of a moment of insight that happened to her overnight. She said that on the previous evening, as we drifted to cafes to enjoy an aperitif or coffee, "wasting" an hour, she felt confused and angry. How could we just sit there, when there was so much to do? She said that in her country, where there are so many needs and the people she works with require so much attention, she has never allowed herself time off. She had always believed that the only right thing to do was to work all the time.

She told us that by morning she realized that nothing had been lost, that leisure is not evil or even amoral but is a normal dimension of life's rhythms. She realizes now, she said, that in her zeal for liberation, she might forget how simply to be with and enjoy people.

Another member of my group, Michael, has been a Catholic priest for twenty-five years, ministering in his native country which is overwhelmingly Buddhist. Michael conveyed to us his growing communion with the Buddhists, a communion born of dialogue and understanding. One of the fruits of this dialogue was an assignment asked of him and a Buddhist monk: they were to walk through some villages in order to gather needed information for some government agencies. The priests' approach to this assignment was to locate the elder in each village and to seek from him the relevant information. One day, they found themselves face-to-face with a very, very old man whose response to their inquiry was to stare at them for a long period of time. Then he said, "I have lived many years, and I never expected to see a Christian priest and Buddhist priest together as you are. You must be brothers." Then he invited them to share a meal with him. The itinerant priests accompanied the old man to his hut where he prepared portions of rice for them. After the meal the old man took a bowl of rice—the only food left in his hut—to a nearby crossroad where he hung the bowl from a low tree branch. Michael asked him what the meaning of this was, and the old man answered, "A man poorer than I will surely come this way." Michael told us that at that moment he heard within him the words of Jesus, "I give my flesh for the life of the world" (John 6:51).

Not only Michael and Regina, but each person in the small groups shared moments of deep insight or change that occurred during the symposium or in the past. I shared that I had come to the symposium feeling guilty that I lived in the First World, a person entwined in the systems that so often manipulate and oppress other parts of the world. What could I say to the Third World? What did I have to offer to Africa or Asia or Latin America? I knew that this guilt had a paralyzing effect, and I expected to be engulfed in even greater feelings of guilt during the symposium. That didn't happen. I found my fellow Christians to be men and women of deep peace, not ruled by hostility or bitterness. Their stance of love had the effect of erasing my feelings of guilt and freeing me to think more clearly about what I could learn from them, and what I could apply to my life, both personally and professionally. Their freedom was contagious. This kind of sharing happened in all the small groups. Each became a community, if only for a week. We walked as friends.

At the end of the symposium, Bishop Henri Teissier, coadjutor Archbishop of Alger and a member of the Council of the Synod in Rome, synthesized the week's work and the many small conversions that happened. He began with a personal reflection, to which he gave the title, "Without true local Christian communities, a Church can disappear."[2] He said:

Let me recall to you the lesson given to us by the history of Christianity in North Africa. In our region today, there are no longer true Local Churches in continuity with the Christian communities of the first centuries of our era. The church of Tertullian, of Cyprian and Augustine, has disappeared, even though it counted up to 700 dioceses at the end of the 5th century. Each of them represented what we would designate today as a Local Church. These communities spoke Latin and formed an integral part of the Roman society, but their environment remained Berber. The Arab conquest eliminated Romanism. Christianity disappeared completely while the Berber culture and language has survived up to our day in most of the mountainous regions. There is every reason to believe that, if Christianity had been inserted into the Berber culture, it would have traversed the centuries as did the Coptic, Syriac,

Assyrian, and Armenian Churches of the Middle East. Thus, without Christian communities truly incarnated into the local reality, the church of a region or a people can disappear.[3]

Bishop Teissier summed up the general consensus that present models of local churches in every part of the world are inappropriate. The need is for churches that are true communities.

> There is a new birth underway and one sign is the birth of basic Christian communities. Under various names, they are multiplying in Latin America, particularly in Brazil, and in Africa and Asia. The growth of these communities does not always spring from the same roots. In Latin America, they are born spontaneously out of small groups of Christians who live in the same place and who confront their concrete needs with the arm of prayer, the word of God, and the evangelical commitment to the poor. In Africa, they respond more to a need for demultiplication of pastoral activity in order to reach each village or each section of the city.[4]

In Europe the decline in the number of priests has led to efforts to find out how the laity can, in a given place, take on the responsibility for the life of the Christian community that no longer has a resident ordained minister. This in turn has led to new forms of Christian community. And while Bishop Teissier did not mention North America in his summing up of basic communities in the life of the local churches, those of us involved with parish renewal felt too the urgency of his words. We agreed with his assessment that out of the diverse experiences of all the participating continents, a somewhat coherent picture was emerging: that of a new way of being church and of living the mission of the church. He pointed out that everywhere we see the growth of people who take seriously their baptismal commitment and who shape that commitment themselves. "It is not a question of constructing another church but much more of experimenting with another manner of being church."[5]

With regard to attitudes of these new forms of church toward the world, Bishop Teissier noted that in some places the basic Christian communities are at an early stage of development where everything is centered on personal spiritual progress or on the liturgical aspect of the community. But in other situations there is an openness of these communities to the problems of society. And in still others, the more fully developed communities, there is the acceptance of a prophetic role in society, not only on the moral level but also on the social level. Finally, in some places there is even training to help the communities function in their prophetic role.

Bishop Teissier articulated for us, participants in the St. Trudo symposium, what we saw and what we heard: that all over the world local churches are moving toward a new way of being (as a communion of services and charisms) and also a new way of living the mission of the church (as a collective and prophetic commitment for the transformation of the world). This is clearly evident in the Third World, but it exists too here and there across North America.

One of the most visible communities of service and prophetic commitment for the transformation of the world is the Sojourners Community. Most people know about the community from their magazine, *Sojourners*, which has one of the largest subscriber audiences of any religious publication. But the community is more than a magazine, much more. Sojourners is people living in Washington, D.C.: people who worship together, protest together, serve the community in which they live, and grow as persons in the process. Sojourners is one expression of the basic Christian community in the context of American culture. Jim Wallis, one of six pastors who serves the community, says it is primarily trying to forge a new spirituality for North Americans, namely a radical conversion of life style and a restoration of shattered covenants. Wallis maintains that shattered covenants abound: with our neighbor, with the poor, with the enemy, with the earth—everywhere.[6] However, the spirituality of Sojourners is not one that negates the world, but one that engages in the struggle to mend, to reconcile, to put the covenants back together again. It is a spirituality centered in community. Wallis gives the example of those persons who have become aware of the dangers of nuclear war and who have worked long and hard at the education of society on this issue, but who see the nation continuing in the arms race. It is natural for them to become embittered, cynical, and despairing. What Willis reminds them and us is that a historic struggle like this requires deep roots and steady resources to nourish the faith that is the essential element in the struggle. But without community one is likely to evade the spiritual work necessary for this kind of nourishing, which is vitally necessary if the prophetic vision is to be kept clear and beckoning.

A sociological scanning of North America reveals that the vision of developed basic Christian communities described by Bishop Teissier at St. Trudo, the vision concretized by Sojourners, is in fact replicated all over the continent. Covenanted communities do exist which are actively committed to working for peace, for attention to the poor, for all the many issues of society that daily confront Christians. Often these communities are extracongregational, gathering and ministering outside of the usual parish structures, and their presence raises a question for the institutional parishes and congregations. Is it possible to experience genuine community there? And if so, how?

The Parish: Communities of Friends
Befriending the World

When I think about the parish I envision a web of interdependent parts which make up the church: the homes of the parishioners, the "domestic church"; the religious education programs, both adult and children's; the pastoral team, that is, the ordained and nonordained who exercise leadership in the parish; and in some cases, the parish school, which hopefully invites the students to a new way of knowing. The key elements in this interdependent web are the people: parents and pastors, teachers and ministers, single adults and children. The image I have of these people and parts is that of communities of friends who in turn befriend the world.

Friendship is one of the central New Testament images. Jesus' ministry happened with and through friends. Peter's confrontational conversations, Mary of Bethany's tenderness, Zaccheus's dinner party, the wedding at Cana, the faithfulness of the beloved disciple—these are the stories of friends and of friendship. And in John's Gospel there is the last discourse of Jesus, his lengthy summing up for himself and for others of the meaning of his life. Facing death, he has sifted and sorted, and what remains for him in these last hours are the essentials. He says to those who have shared this final Passover meal with him that he will not call them servants. "I call you friends," he says. How does one describe a friend? And what would a community of friends look like?

Aelred of Rievaulx, a twelfth-century monk, writes that a friend is "the companion of your soul to whose spirit you join and attach your own; to whom you entrust yourself as to another self, from whom you hide nothing, from whom you fear nothing."[7] Aelred, like Jesus, sees the explicit connection among friendship, love, and unity, so that it is natural for Aelred to say "God is friendship." I think it is important to remember that this is not a vague, sentimental statement, but carries with it all the concrete ways in which people interdependently share life with one another.

While this order of friendship is at the heart of marriage, the nature of the love is such that it spills out over the children, over other family members, and even over those outside the home. One can see, then, the possibilities for Christians. From the beginning others looked at the communities of Christians and saw in them a depth of love that was remarkable. And also from the beginning the inner friendship impelled the communities to move beyond the natural ties of flesh and blood and the divine ties of friendship to embrace others, not only those similar in taste and culture and education but also very different others, as did Frank Laubach to the Moros, as does Teresa of Calcutta to the most abandoned.

Contemporary Communities: Qualities to Cultivate

The issue before the local churches in the First World (Europe as well as North America) is how to form mature communities, communities that respond to the particular cultural conditions of Western society, communities moving toward their prophetic and pastoral role vis-à-vis this society, communities of friends befriending the world.

Natural groups within a congregation are places to begin this formation. Parish councils, education committees, service projects, parent-teacher organizations—all have the potential for becoming true communities rather than task groups only. But we need to study and reflect upon the qualities to be nurtured in these developing communities. We need to ponder the profile of community.

One way to describe community is to say what it is not. It is not a new elitist enclave which reinforces the cultural and social biases of the members. Quite the opposite, true community helps us to see and to be free of the cultural addictions that largely run our lives. It does so through a number of dynamics. Among these dynamics are four which seem to me to be fundamental in the shaping of a community of friends.

I do not see these dynamics as strictly separate from each other, but rather as different aspects of the reality of Christian friendship. I see all the actors within the parish web, the adults and the children, the clergy and the laity, participating in this formation in some way. I believe Aelred is right about friendship. It is God's transforming power.

The Cultivation of Relationships

The first dynamic in the formation of Christian communities, and perhaps the foundational one, is the attention given to the cultivation of relationships. In an essay, "Liberating the Divine Energy,"[8] Rosemary Haughton speaks of relationships as the central ingredient in the establishment of the new social order that was the heart of Jesus' legacy to us. She points out that key to this new order was Jesus' sensitivity to actual people, concrete individuals in whom he perceived the operation of the same divine energy that was his own motivating power. In her words, "He knew people not only as acted upon by divine power but as sources of it." What did he say to the healed and the reconciled? Your faith has saved you. Somehow in the transaction between Jesus and the other divine energy was released. Haughton admits that Jesus' compassion was an essential agent, but she reminds us, so was the faith of the seeker. Her point is that the transformation took place—often a psychophysical transformation—not in isolation but in encounter. What the people of Jesus' time and culture saw happening over and over again were new breakthroughs of God, and although Jesus seems to have tried to contain the phenomenon within the traditional structures of his religion, Haughton asserts, "it could not be done." A new social organism was required. She notes that this has been the experience through the centuries of those who have recaptured the vision that Jesus had and lived out. They often find themselves in conflict with the institutions that claim to represent the divine energy, and so new communities are born. This is demonstrated in the rise of religious orders, in lay movements, and in basic Christian communities, all of which may be connected to the church but which are clearly new forms within the overarching institution.

The focus of community is the same focus that Jesus had, namely relationship, that "space between" where human beings are able to become themselves as known to each other. Such exchanges between people occur in an environment of compassion which is the antithesis of dominance, competition, or manipulation. Again, marriage is an example of the kind of ongoing encounter I'm talking about. Something powerful happens between the spouses. Creativity is released; personalities are transformed under the influence of each other; something new emerges from the energy shared between wife and husband. The "new" may be as concrete and unrepeatable as a human person, or it may be more intangible: the deepening of hope, the firming of faith, the crystallizing of active love in one's work, vocation, or mission. As marriage is a community of equals, so must be the local church, if it is to be a community of friends. This appreciation of equality before God presumes coming to know one another deeply. Practicality, of course, limits the size of the community. Because of this, parishes as we know them may need to be restructured into many gatherings or communities of friends.

This attentiveness to relationships will certainly mean a new kind of listening: an attentiveness to the unspoken as well as to the spoken word, an attentiveness to persons throughout the entire parish. Those in positions of pastoral and educational responsibility will need to foster dialogue, the new kind of talking that John Coleman speaks of and that I discussed in the chapter on work. Parents, teachers, and pastors will need to talk with one another about their agreed-upon Christian values and about how those values are lived out in the many expressions of church that constitute the totality of the parish, including the school and the home. For example, I expect regular dialogue would be needed between home and school about the Christian value of cooperation versus competition. If the parish school is to be a place where excellence is not the same as beating someone else out, then parents (who work in a competitive society) will have to be helped to deal with their own expectations regarding school. Parents, teachers, pastors, and staff will have to spend time listening to each other, and listening to God, in order to make cooperation rather than competition the guiding principle.

Respect for the Truth

The second dynamic I've identified as important in the formation of community is respect for the truth. Respect for the truth includes the willingness to face the truth about oneself, something that is virtually impossible to do without community in some form. Parents know that children help us to become ever more truthful persons. It is not only that we are called upon over and over again to state the objective truth about one thing or another but we are called by our children to deal with our personal truth as well.

One of the most moving examples of parental truthfulness occurs in the memoirs of Eugenia Ginzburg. In *Within the Whirlwind,* the second volume of her memoirs, she tells the reason for writing the details of her many years of political imprisonment under Stalin. It was simply that the truth be known. Her son, who was only four when she was imprisoned, was directly responsible for this enormous undertaking. When he was sixteen they were reunited in Siberia. Their first night together they recited poems until the dawn came, discovering the deep and unbroken bond between them. As the sun appeared in the sky, her son asked her what her life had been like all those years when they were apart. She decided then to tell him only the truth (she said it could not be the whole truth because no one knew the whole truth); she would not hide anything from him. That decision was the beginning of her memoirs.[9] We see here one kind of release of divine energy, that generated between mother and son, yielding an extraordinary work of art.

Like Ginzburg we all have some personal truth set in a social context of one kind or another. Who is there to ask what has happened to us and what have we learned as a result? Who is there to ask us to name the hope in our work, in our neighborhoods, in our country, in our churches? These are the kinds of questions that grow up in a community of friends. Furthermore, they suggest an adult education agenda that will help the people themselves to shape the questions they need to get at the truth of their lives.

Language is one of the principal conveyors of truth. Communities of friends can help one another recognize the kind of language the church, individually and collectively, speaks to ourselves, to our children, to the world. Unless someone brings it to our attention we may remain unconscious and unable to take a stand against distorted and cliche-ridden language. Friends care enough to do so. Friends will alert us to the inconsistency in calling the MX, which is capable of killing millions of persons, the "peacemaker." The community of friends can strengthen us to refuse to allow discriminatory language of any kind to flourish in our environment because that, too, distorts the reality of a person.

In community we learn that language carries consequences. We see the vivid truth of this in the work of Athol Fugard, a South African playwright. In his play, *Master Harold and the Boys,* Fugard uncovers the racism that dwells undisturbed in all of us. Harold is a seventeen-year-old white young man, nicknamed Hally, whose mother owns and operates a small bar and restaurant and whose father is an alcoholic, paralyzed, and for the most part, bedridden. Hally is friends with two "boys," black men who work for his mother and who have known Hally since he was a tiny child. One of the boys, Sam, is Hally's special friend. They are involved with each other at several levels: intellectually, spiritually, and socially. Sam is, in some ways, a surrogate father or mentor to Hally. It is evident that theirs is a close relationship, the kind that is uniquely possible between a child and a loving adult.

Then, in one moment of irrepressible anger at his alcoholic father, Hally, who cannot or will not confront his father, turns on Sam; Hally insults his color and insists that Sam call him from now on not by the familiar name of friendship, Hally, but by the name that signifies the societal roles of dominance and subordination. Hally demands to be called Master Harold. Sam, in his wisdom, knows that once spoken, that title of mastery over another human being will set in motion consequences that cannot be reversed.[10]

Readers or watchers of the play are given a mirror in which they see reflected the isms that divide all of us. Because we are so clever at rationalizing and defending ourselves, we need Athol Fugards to create images that can break through our self-justifications. Once we can see, we can repent. Some say that the reluctance of many religious institutions publicly to repent for the treatment of blacks or women or other marginalized persons can be traced to self-blindness not unlike that of Hally. While the gospel enjoins us to bring to light all that is hidden, we are given no clue as to how long this may take. Athol Fugard suggests it is a long and arduous struggle.

It seems to me that without the presence of genuine community where trust, accountability, and courage are evident, the journey to truth can be successfully evaded. I suspect that it is possible to live for many years in a parish and not be prodded to face this freeing truth. It is challenge enough for parishes to look at their community-building efforts.

Inner Work

The third dynamic of community life which I have identified is what I call inner work. A critical question today concerns our capacity to open the doorways of the spiritual world and then to walk through those doorways toward the center where God alone is. I have heard people say that the parish usually does a creditable job of passing on the tradition and the moral teaching of the church, but it does not seem as well equipped to help people enter into the direct, experiential knowledge of God. Yet, theologian Karl Rahner contends that "the Christian of the future will be a mystic or he will not exist at all." He goes on to say:

> The ultimate conviction and decision of faith comes in the last resort, not from pedagogic indoctrination from outside, supported by public opinion in secular society or in the Church, nor from a merely rational argumentation of fundamental theology, but from the experience of God, of God's spirit, of God's freedom, bursting out of the very heart of human existence and able to be really experienced there, even though this experience cannot be wholly a matter for reflection or be verbally objectified.[11]

Inner work does not require a degree in spirituality. You may remember Ruby Bridges, the six-year-old child in the 60s, who day after day walked past heckling, menacing mobs in order to attend the newly desegregated New Orleans elementary school. The white children had been withdrawn, and Ruby was alone each day in the classroom with her reluctant white teacher. Reluctant though she was, the teacher could not help but note the little girl's courage. The teacher spoke of watching Ruby walking along with the federal marshals, while the people shouted obscenities and threats at her. One of the marshals told Ruby's teacher that the little girl had more courage than he'd seen anywhere, even on the battlefield. He said she didn't even seem afraid. When asked about fear, Ruby would shift the ground of discussion and say, "I do what my granny says. I keep on praying."[12]

Ruby is an example of the moment-by-moment trust in God that even the gates of hell cannot prevail against. Her granny, who was surely her friend, empowered her in ways not unlike that recorded in Acts. But with her was also the praying, singing, caring black community, Ruby's people, God's people, the community of friends.

We see that same inner strength in a young Jewish woman who lived in Amsterdam during the time when the Holocaust was closing in. The diaries of Etty Hillesum, now published under the title *An Interrupted Life*, tell of her hard, interior work to move beyond self-interest to radical freedom. With the help of a psychologist friend and a close circle of young intellectuals, Etty grows from a young woman centered on her own emotional, intellectual, and physical problems, a person who claims no knowledge of God, to one who near the end of her young life (she died at twenty-seven) addresses God in this way:

> Dear God, these are anxious times. Tonight, for the first time I lay in the dark with burning eyes as scene after scene of human suffering passed before me. I shall promise you one thing, God, just one very small thing. I shall never burden my today with cares about tomorrow, although that takes some practice. Each day is sufficient unto itself.

And then she goes on to write to God in a tone of absolute honesty and piercing insight.

> One thing is becoming increasingly clear to me: that You cannot help us [the Jews], but that we must help You to help ourselves. And that is all we can manage these days, and also all that really matters: that we safeguard that little piece of you, God, in ourselves. And perhaps in others as well.[13]

How is it that one comes to such fearless truthfulness? I believe that the community is an indispensable element in assisting one on the inner search and supporting the inner work. But a significant part of that interior effort is time given to solitude and silence. It is there that one becomes attuned to the invisible, and it is there that one can turn anytime. When Etty thinks of her future in the camps, she reassures herself: "I keep finding myself in prayer. And that is something I shall always be able to do, even in the smallest space—pray." I think one of the functions of community is to support its members in the sabbath experience, the resting in God, the aloneness, the experience of space where one's true self stands free.

This spiritual inner work, if it is authentic, is not self-indulgent. There is not a shred of sentimentality or self-inflation in either Ruby or Etty. When the child, Ruby, faces the daily violence of hate-filled adults, she just keeps on praying. For Ruby school meant not defying the mob (that's what she had to do to get to school) but learning her letters and her numbers. For Etty what matters as much as her spiritual insights are the details of everyday life: walks along the Amsterdam canal, the smell of jasmine in her yard, the view outside her bedroom window, the man she loves and with whom she shares a bottle of wine or hot cocoa.

In the chapter on spirituality I indicated the extraparochial pilgrimages that laypeople were engaged in, the diverse ways that the hungry are fed and the spiritually thirsty given drink. However, the question remains about the capacity and the willingness of the parish to provide resources within the usual structures so that men and women, and yes, children are encouraged to stay with the spiritual quest.

Vocation and Mission

The fourth dynamic that is of the very substance of community life is the discerning of one's personal vocation and the community's corporate ministry in fidelity to the mission of Christ. Clarity regarding one's vocation requires an intentional turning inward, a listening in a nondefensive way to the loving truth that abides within. This listening is, of course, part of the inner work that patiently scrapes away the defenses that block self-knowledge. But what one hears in the darkness, in the silence, must be shared in the light. And that is one of the main purposes of community: to be the safe place to articulate the content of one's heart, a place to test the call, to be supported in the call, or to change, if that seems indicated. It is in the context of community that we can see how our work serves as a modest but responsible contribution to the general welfare. I've already talked about my daughter's sense of vocation to the theater and how she sees her work linked to the common good, but how about government workers, garbage collectors, and public safety workers, farmers and street cleaners, teachers and store clerks? Do they know that their work, their vocations, are invaluable contributions to the whole? Probably not. We all need to be reminded, inspired, and encouraged to believe and apply the words of Martin Luther King, Jr.: "If it falls to your lot to be a street sweeper, sweep streets as Michelangelo carved marble. Sweep streets as

Shakespeare wrote plays. Sweep streets so well that all the hosts of heaven will have to say, 'Here lives a great street sweeper who did his job well.' "[14] We need community to keep us listening, both to the call and to the affirmation of the call.

The role of community is not only to heighten our sense of personal vocation, important as that is. The community of friends is further characterized by a sense of mission, participation in and responsibility for that which Jesus referred to as the kingdom of God: those norms of justice, peace, righteousness, and freedom in the secular arenas. On the feast of Rosh Hashana this year (1985), the Jewish Theological Seminary of America ran an ad in the *Washington Post* which read in part, "A man in Jerusalem hears the battering rams at the gates. He fears that his world is doomed. In this moment of despair, God tells him to buy a homestead. Why does the Bible tell this story about the prophet Jeremiah? To remind us that even in the worst of times, one must have faith in the future, and act on it." The ad goes on to address the reader, both Jew and Gentile, "Judaism has this to say: Is the world coming apart? Then fix it. It's your job. Commit to it and fix it. The world is perfectible and people's actions are the only way it will be perfected. Time will pass, and in the time we have, we will make choices. Don't we really know what we want for our families, our neighborhood, our cities, for our nations, and for the world? This year, choose to fix your world." This full-page ad celebrating the Jewish New Year has captured the spirit of mission. This is what Christian communities are ultimately called to do: to choose to commit to fixing the world, or at least some small part of it. That's what the literacy councils do all over the world. That's what the hospice movement does. That's what the justice and peace organizations of all kinds choose to do. That's what action cleanup for rivers and lakes does. That's what basic Christian communities all over the world are doing. That's what parish communities of friends can do. This is the work of the gathered church.

A member of the Bruderhof community in Germany spoke about mission during the dark days of 1932. He said:

The colossal need facing humankind in this hour of history makes it urgent to show a new way. The time is here for the communal Church to be a light on the lampstand, a city on a hill (Matt. 5:14, 15). The reality of the God-given life among us must affect many and finally all people. The time is here when the message of God's unity, justice, and brotherhood in His Kingdom must be spread abroad. But we are exceedingly weak and our numbers are small, very small, when we think of the magnitude of this calling. . . .

We cannot evade the call of Jesus or the impulse of our hearts. It is a call that goes out to all, especially to all the needy. And when the misery reaches such a pitch as we see around us today, the call of Jesus becomes all the more insistent and pressing—more so than ever before. 'Go ye out into all the world' (Mark 16:15). Go out, get to work! Call the people and gather them in! Now is the hour![15]

He spoke over fifty years ago. Much of what this member of the Bruderhof said is applicable today. But one thing is exceedingly clear: without community we can and do evade the call of Jesus.

Befriending the World

Is it possible for Christians to think of ourselves as citizens of the world? I think so.

A parish that lives its life in the pattern of communities of friends, that is, intentionally given to developing the inner life (friendship with God) and the outer life of mission (which is what God's friends do), will be naturally guiding God's children toward world citizenship, toward the unity that Jesus prayed and longed for. Children who live and grow in communities of friends will know that they belong to God and to the world so loved by God. Clearly, there are many difficulties ahead as we attempt to befriend each other and the world. We are a nation that prizes individualism and values our private lives.[16]

There is a challenge here—and an agenda for the present and the future. This agenda belongs to the many different ministries of the church. It is a collaborative agenda, which will require the pastoral leadership to begin with themselves to enter into the formation of a community of friends. By the pastoral leadership I mean the ordained and the lay staff and leadership of a parish. But community, if it is truly that and not merely an imitation, will be open to others: to families, to the divorced, to the elderly, to single adults, to the citizens of the civil community, to the refugee, to the imprisoned, and to the impoverished. The wider community of friends will know about and reach out to the barrios of South America, the gulags of the East, the homelands of South Africa.

This is a doable agenda. What is needed is the willingness to change and to make wineskins for the new wine now fermenting in our churches.

Conclusion

The prophetic lived and living questions that inform the laity's life can all be addressed in the experience of community. The spiritual yearning of men and women, the experience of marriage and family with its analogues for the wider church, the meaning of work and the readiness for mission, the special gifts of women for the church and for the world—all these are the substance of community. It is the role of the institutional church, I believe, to lay aside all that would block or delay the good news of community formation.

NOTES

1. The Beguinage is a cluster of houses where, during the Middle Ages, a community of laywomen called the Beguines lived. The Beguines took monastic vows, and many were workers engaged in lace making, tutoring, caring for the sick, etc. Their communities were mostly found in the Netherlands and Belgium.

2. Bishop Henri Teissier, "So That True Christian Communities May Grow," a paper presented at the Intercontinental Symposium on the Local Church at St. Trudo Abbey, Bruges, Belgium.

3. Ibid.

4. Ibid.

5. Ibid.

6. Jim Wallis in a presentation to the Ecumenical Institute of Spirituality, January 1984.

7. Aelred of Rievaulx, *Spiritual Friendship* (Kalamazoo, Mich.: Cistercian Publications, 1977).

8. Rosemary Haughton, "Liberating the Divine Energy," in *Living With Apocalypse* (San Francisco: Harper & Row, 1984).

9. Eugenia Ginzburg, *Within the Whirlwind* (New York: Harcourt Brace Jovanovich, 1981).

10. Athol Fugard, *Master Harold and the Boys* (New York: Random House, 1982).

11. Karl Rahner, *Concern for the Church* (New York: Crossroad, 1981); quoted in Tolbert McCarroll, *Guiding God's Children* (Mahwah, N.J.: Paulist Press, 1983), 157.

12. "The Hero Without and Within," *New Oxford Review* 52, 2 (March 1985).

13. Etty Hillesum, *An Interrupted Life* (New York: Pantheon Books, 1983), 151.

14. Martin Luther King, Jr., in an address to street sweepers, April 1968.

15. Eberhard Arnold, "The Gathered Life," *Sojourners* (May 1984).

16. Cf. Robert Bellah, Richard Madsen, William M. Sullivan, Ann Swidler and Steven M. Tipton, *Habits of the Heart: Individualism and Commitment in American Life* (Berkeley: Univ. of California Press, 1985).

FOR FURTHER READING

Hug, James E., S.J., ed. *Training the Spirit: Communities, Social Action and Theological Reflections.* Mahwah, N.J.: Paulist Press, 1983.

Kemp, Raymond B. *A Journey in Faith: An Experience of the Catechumate.* New York: Wm. H. Sadlier, 1979.

Palmer, Parker. *The Company of Strangers.* New York: Crossroad Pub. Co., 1981.

Whitehead, Evelyn Eaton, and James D. Whitehead. *Community of Faith: Models and Strategies for Developing Christian Communities.* New York: Seabury Press, 1982.

Afterword

SOMEONE ONCE SAID that by fifty years of age everyone gets the face he or she deserves. I assume that the meaning of this statement is that life has etched its indelible marks there and that each of us participates in the etching. I have noticed that some people are far more beautiful in their later years than they were in the full bloom of youth. Their faces soften. Their eyes seek, yet are peaceful. They smile frequently, as if grateful for some surprise or gift. They speak with utmost respect to others. Their faces are open, expecting the best from the world. They are truly beautiful.

I think the church shares in these personal attributes. After all, the church is comprised of people. In our time, I see the face of the church always beautiful, even when suffering, changing. As with individual persons, the change is generated by interactions with new people and new situations. The lives of laypeople, who comprise the largest segment of the church, are taking new shapes, and this phenomenon is enough to change the shape of the church's visage.

I have argued in these pages that the laity's quest for and experience of spirituality are factors in this change. People want more, or so it seems. They want some direct experience of God, and they often have found that available to them outside the boundaries of the parish. This presses the parish to look at its own spirituality.

New patterns of marriage and family life are also affecting the church in several ways. One is within the more personal space of the home, which is itself a church, the "domestic church." As Christ's prayer for unity is realized in ecumenical and interfaith marriages, as parents live

117

consciously through death and resurrection moments, as families discover that they bless one other, evangelize through the generosity of their lives, and minister through their work, the whole church body adjusts its posture and persona.

I have particularly emphasized the centrality of the workplace as a site for ministry and mission, but I have also contended that Christians are called to even more distant frontiers. They are called to some form of intentional mission that is pure gift. Either alone or with others gathered in Christ's name, I have maintained that our vocation includes donating our giftedness in the "extra mile," perhaps to fix the world where it needs fixing, as the Rosh Hashana message of the Jewish Theological Seminary stated.

The changing role of women, in both society and church, is present as a major force in the reshaping of the church's presentation of itself to the world. For many, many people the credibility of all the churches is linked with their capacity to honor the principles of equality and interdependence between men and women. Women want a different role in the church, one that is at least as respectful of their experience and insights as is their emerging role in other institutions of society.

Finally, it is my sincere belief that these issues or questions can only be honestly dealt with in a genuine community, a gathering in which one is known and respected, a gathering which keeps alive the essential message of the gospel: we are a mission people.

While the principal focus of this book has been the laity, I think it is only fair to state that clergy and vowed religious are also engaged in prophetic questioning. In the Catholic church, for example, the bishops have raised the issues of the morality of a nuclear arms race and the relationship of U.S. economic policy to the common good—surely moral issues.[1] We all can name clergy and vowed religious whose lives are a continual prophetic witness. Ultimately, of course, it is the church as church that is the prophetic voice, calling all of us, as well as the world, to deeper and deeper conversion. At the Bruges symposium, Bishop Teissier asked: "Is it not the local church as a whole (clergy and laity) that must share the prophetic Word and the action for the Kingdom? The local church is a human cell and, as such, a reality of the world, as well as an active sign of the Kingdom and, as such, involved in the evangelical transformation of realities."[2]

It will not do for laity and clergy to go their separate ways to the extent that they never touch each other's lives except in the most superficial ways. The mission of the church, which is the pastoral care of the world, needs the attention of *all* the church if it is to bring to bear upon the world the fullness of divine energy. But alongside this primary mission, there is needed a sustained internal renewal. The laity's prophetic questions are an invitation to dialogue, a necessary ingredient for all reflection and conversion. Hopefully, the church close to home, namely the parish, will be the site of dialogue, for that's the place where Christians gather, the place where church matters most, the place where people have a chance of incarnating the gospel in everyday life.

Jesus compared the kingdom of God to yeast which a woman mixes in with flour until it permeates the dough. Little bits of yeast everywhere allowing the dough to rise and become delicious bread that is both nourishing and enjoyable. A friend of mine thinks of this as the laity's parable. And so it is, for we are everywhere: in offices, in schools, in scientific laboratories, in the military, in hospitals, in theaters and orchestras, in public transportation, in the media— scattered throughout the dough of the world. But as I indicated at the beginning of this book, the laity are not passively being kneaded, but are themselves agents of change, the stirrers and the mixers. The result is an atmosphere of anticipation, a sense of preparing for the Lord's banquet.

NOTES

1. Cf. *The Challenge of Peace: God's Promise and our Response;* and the *Pastoral Letter on Catholic Social Teaching and the U.S. Economy.*

2. Bishop Henri Teissier, "So That True Christian Communities May Grow."